U-BOAT H

BY THE SAME AUTHOR

U-Boats Destroyed:
The Effect of Anti-Submarine Warfare 1914-1918

U-Boat Intelligence:
Admiralty Intelligence Division and the Defeat of the U-Boats 1914-1918

Published by Periscope Publishing Ltd.
www.periscopepublishing.com

U–BOAT HUNTERS

Code Breakers, Divers and the Defeat of the U-Boats, 1914—1918

ROBERT M. GRANT

PERISCOPE PUBLISHING
PENZANCE

Published in 2003 by
Periscope Publishing Ltd.
33 Barwis Terrace
Penzance
Cornwall TR18 2AW

www.periscopepublishing.com

A CIP record for this book is available from the British Library

ISBN No 1-904381-15-4

Printed in England by Anthony Rowe Ltd
Eastbourne

CONTENTS

ILLUSTRATIONS

Photos published with the kind permissions of: The Imperial War Museum, Royal Navy Submarine Museum, Nick Baker (Historical Diving Society), Innes McCartney, John Hammond and U-Boot Archiv.

PREFACE

The submarine, first fully employed during the Great War of 1914-1918, nearly achieved victory for Germany after it was aimed more against merchant shipping than the Royal Navy. The British, especially, and the French had to develop new means to hold the U-boat in check. Since submarines had to communicate with their bases, not only as they returned home but also during their cruises, the interception and decryption of their radio signals proved extremely important. At the beginning both British and German forces cut cables all over the world, but they soon realized that reading radio messages was more vital.

This book is a study of some of the ways in which the Royal Navy was able to decipher German U-boat signals in what was known as "Room 40" in the Admiralty's Old Building, especially after divers found ciphers in wrecks sunk in coastal waters or ground searchers found them in Zeppelins. The question then arises: What use in action was made of the information acquired? Most information entered the "data bank," usefully pointing to ordinary procedures and the routes U-boats took. Occasionally, however, when the larger submarines far outside the North Sea attempted to meet, British forces tried to take part in their rendezvous. Their hopes were not often fulfilled but sometimes, dramatic encounters took place. Of course action and intelligence formed aspects of the same events. Analysis suggests separating them, but the story often requires us to consider both aspects at the same time.

These famed U-boats and their opponents were of great interest after the Great War of 1914-1918. In 1936 I was able to study documents in the Office of Naval Records and Library in Washington and later to publish three articles in the United States Naval Institute Proceedings. In 1960 an old friend at Annapolis, Captain R. W. Daly, USCGR, made it possible to work in the World War I U-boat records in the Tambach collection. The Germans were about to destroy their naval archives toward the end of the second war, but the British captured them at Tambach in central Germany, thanks in part to urging by Ian Fleming[1]. In London the Americans made microfilms of most of them and I was given access to these, now in the National Archives at Washington. My first naval book, *U-Boats Destroyed* (Putnam, London, 1964), was largely based on them. I am grateful to those who helped my earlier research: especially Admirals Ernest M. Eller, R. R. Belknap, A. S. Carpender, R. B. Carney, and F. Kent Loomis; and Commander P. K. Kemp of the Royal Navy. The air historian Dr. Douglas Robinson also continued to encourage and advise.

For my second book, *U-Boat Intelligence* (Putnam, 1969), Rear-Admiral P. N. Buckley of the Naval Historical Branch of the Admiralty, encouraged by the late Admiral Sir William James (who had been in charge of Room 40, dealing with codes and ciphers, in 1918), gave me access to British documents now in the Public Record Office at Kew in London. I was also helped by H. F. Langley and J. D. Brown of the Historical Branch, as well as Professor Arthur Marder.

After the second book, more documents opened up, especially at Kew, and I have continued searching in them during the last thirty years. The most important of them contain records of intercepted signals, Admiralty telegrams with orders based on such signals, and files on divers and their discoveries in U-boat wrecks off the British and Irish coasts. The cryptographer David Kahn lent me microfilms of French reports, while the British naval historians Anthony Sainsbury and the late Patrick Beesly helped and encouraged me to continue. I owe a great deal to successive Directors of Naval History in Washington, especially Dr. Dean Allard, and to their opposite numbers in London. I have also had very helpful correspondence with C.-H. Ankarberg of Stockholm, Sweden. Most recently Dwight Messimer, author of *Verschollen*, not only produced a valuable study but directed me (after my daughter Susan) to the indispensable reports on the Web from modern divers. The aid of Innes McCartney, U-boat researcher, diver, and publisher, has proved invaluable.

Today important collections of documents are found in the National Archives in Washington and the Public Record Office in London, though one should add the Post Office Archives in London for matters related to underwater cables as well as the Department of Defence Records in Ottawa. A word on the references seems in order. I cite German documents by the PG numbers under which the British and the Americans filed them[2]. Since they are arranged by subject and chronology, no more precise reference is needed. A similar chronological arrangement obtains in the various Admiralty (ADM 137) and Admiralty Salvage (ADM 116) files in the Public Record Office at Kew, London. These are cited by file and document, as are American documents at the National Archives in Washington and Canadian documents in Ottawa.

The book is dedicated to my old friend Captain Anthony B. Sainsbury, RNR, because of his constant concern and help.

Robert M. Grant
Divinity School, University of Chicago

I

INFORMATION

1. Revelations

Immediately after the Great War a young American ensign who had served on Admiral Sims's staff in London was the first to discuss what the British had known of U-boat movements. He explained that radio signals intercepted every night revealed the exact position of most submarines at sea, and added that they were always in code and "might, or might not, be eventually deciphered by the Admiralty." It made no difference, for direction finders could determine the direction or bearing of a signal "to a fraction of a degree." Leighton went on to say that

> the Admiralty took the greatest care that this method of locating submarines should not be discovered by the enemy, for the authorities regarded it as the greatest secret in their possession; and there is no evidence to show that the Germans ever did discover it."[3]

He obviously thought that the secret of direction finding, then called "radiogoniometry," no longer needed keeping, while he correctly shielded the triumphs of decryption.

The same year in Britain, however, when Julian Corbett began publishing his *Naval Operations* as part of the *History of the Great War based on Official Documents* the Admiralty supplied a notice for the first page.

> The Lords Commissioners of the Admiralty have given the Author access to official documents in the preparation of this work, but they are in no way responsible for his reading or presentation of the facts as stated.

The notice was repeated in each of the four later volumes, and in 1931 Corbett's successor Henry Newbolt added a preface of his own, mentioning papers "retained by some branch of the Admiralty."[4] He did not say what they were, but they certainly included the documents on which we have relied for this study.

The Admiralty believed that the less outsiders knew about naval intelligence the better. After all, toward the end of the war some German officers had been deeply impressed by how much the British knew, for example on occasions when they intercepted German forces in the North Sea. Admiral von Hipper is a prime example. He was "particularly disappointed that on November 17 [1917] the Englishmen had been actually on the very spot -- and in superior force -- where the raid of the German cruisers had begun." Indeed, he claimed that "the war at sea made it absolutely obvious that some secret power was working against us, and it was thus inevitable that earnest men should rack their brains as to how the evil should be fought and how they should make sure that things which ought to be kept secret should in fact be kept secret." This ominous statement is based on the fact that the British somehow knew about German minesweeping in the Bight. "We could be perfectly certain from the behaviour of British submarines that the enemy had an amazingly accurate knowledge of the passages we had cleared through the mine-fields."[5] Where did the knowledge come from?

For many years after World War I the same mantle of secrecy lay over the divers who searched the wrecks of U-boats sunk off the British coast. Stories about them were severely censored and intentionally garbled. The first faintly reliable account came from Diver E. C. Miller, who described searches for seven U-boats in his article "A War Secret" in the *Saturday Evening Post* for October 23, 1926. He had been made MBE in the New Year Honours List of 1919 and his DSC was gazetted on July 10 of that year "for distinguished services in connection with dangerous and important salvage work." He was the leading diver in a team led by the more famous Lt. Cdr. G. C. C. Damant (formerly Inspector of Diving) that salved gold worth five million pounds from the steamer *Laurentic*, mined off Lough Swilly, Ireland.[6] According to Damant, after September 1917 "our party and their equipment were engaged on other but more exciting work through the summer of 1918."[7] The "more exciting work" was the exploration of U-boat wrecks.

In the *Post* article Miller described his first search, that of a U-boat supposedly sunk by gunfire off the coast of Kent. He got into the wreck abaft the conning tower and worked his way forward to the officers' quarters, where he found "two secret codes used in the German Navy, together with the one used to communicate to the High Seas Fleet." Loose sheets provided part of a plan of a minefield laid only three days earlier and other papers showed that the U-boat had left port only thirty-six hours before she was sunk. Then there was another boat with a strong box containing "a set of new codes, a blueprint of the plan of the vessel, and plans of two complete new minefields in the North Sea." From then on, says the reporter, "Diver Miller descended to every sunken U-boat that could be located.... No fewer than sixty sunken German submarines did Miller explore." In fact, none of Miller's stories was historically exact, since all were disclosed "with official permission"; he left the work of other successful salvage experts out of account; and the figure sixty was inflated. The general impression he gave, however, was right.

Five years later H. C. Bywater, naval correspondent of the *Daily Telegraph*, joined H. C. Ferraby to produce *Strange Intelligence*. Their thirteenth chapter dealt with "the men who heard the U-boats talk," and simply ascribed information to two sources: directional interception (which gave only "approximate positions") and the decipherment of call signs, important for identifying boats and confirming "the accuracy of all [the] other information." At first the call signs followed a regular pattern and could be made out without difficulty. Toward the end of the war a new principle was introduced, but the signs could be read in three weeks. In his foreword to the second printing (1934), Admiral Sir Reginald Hall reassured the Admiralty about the authors and their book. "What they disclose can now do no harm either to the public service or individuals."[8] He was also thinking of his own proposed memoirs, whose publication the Admiralty had already vetted and vetoed.

In 1932 Bywater provided further revelations in his book *Their Secret Purposes*. One story told how a British submarine met two U-cruisers at their rendezvous off the Spanish coast and torpedoed one of them because of "papers taken out of a German submarine which had been depth-charged and promptly salved."[9] Since the only U-boat thus torpedoed was *U154*, on May 10, 1918, the other submarine, depth-charged and salved, should be easy to identify. Such is not the case because the boat never existed. The radio signals that gave away the place and time of the U-cruisers' meeting could be read because the British already could read the cipher.

Bywater also told the story of "another discovery of secret papers [that] led to the greatest haul of U-boats made during the whole war." After *UB450*, which he calls "a fictitious designation,"[10] was depth-charged "off the Durham coast" on July 19, 1918, Admiralty Salvage proceeded to raise the wreck. Inside it were "a log-book, signal codes, documents and charts." Lines in red ink on a chart of "the home seas" indicated routes taken by five U-boats (numbers noted) when bound north of Scotland for the Atlantic, and most of them showed "safe resting-places on the bottom of the sea." This chart soon brought results. "Within a comparatively brief time after the salving of *UB450* -- eleven weeks to be precise -- every one of the five submarines had been accounted for," by mines or patrols.[11]

Bywater's account drew sharp criticism from the German official historian Admiral Spindler, who pointed out that *UB110* was salved on October 4, while no U-boats had sailed from Zeebrugge after September 16. The five vessels mentioned therefore could not have passed from Flanders through the North Sea around Scotland, and the U-boat war ended two weeks after the boat was raised. In addition, the Admiralty had assured Spindler that the charts aboard *UB110* contained no entry that could have led to the destruction of other U-boats.[12]   When her commander, W. Fürbringer, was interrogated he insisted that he "never rested on the bottom, and though smaller submarines sometimes lie on the bottom during the day, this practise is not universal and many officers are strongly averse to it." In fact, however, *UB110* on her way to Zeebrugge had rested on the bottom south of the Schouwen Bank in two locations, while the charts of several other Flanders U-boats indicate safe resting places at the bottom of the sea. For instance, in May *UB108* pointed to locations for lying on the bottom north of the Schouwen Bank, while her June charts contain notes on areas off the British coast east of Smiths Knoll and northeast of the Outer Dowsing. In August *UB104's* chart marks resting places just off Souter Point and just north of Flamborough Head, while *UB112* lay on the bottom just off Whitby, close to the coast. Perhaps such information did lead the British to watch specific locations along the East Coast and toward the Northern Barrage. It seems unlikely that documents were extracted from *UB110* before she was finally raised, however, since as late as September 22 Hall issued orders that

> investigation and search work inside the vessel, except as required to make her float, is not to take place as the object being aimed at is to first of all repair the hull damage without delay...[13]

His order could mean that the necessary search had already taken place but this is improbable. The wreck had been found July 29. "After this operations were suspended until August 10th when Cdr.[C. J.] Wheeler and diving party returned." There seems to have been no pressure for finding documents, and the chart Bywater described cannot have led to U-boat sinkings.

In 1939 there appeared a very discreet biography of Sir Alfred Ewing, the first director of "Room 40" by his son A. W. Ewing, helped by Admiral Sir William James, formerly Hall's deputy.[14]   As an engineering student Ewing had tested cables in England and Uruguay. In 1914 as Director of Naval Education he became involved in cryptography, though the book reveals few details. Even so, in 1932 the Admiralty had refused permission for him to publish his own account. They also denied it to Hall in 1933 when he put together five chapters of his memoirs and took them to the Admiralty. He was told, "publication should be withheld for the time being."[15]

More reliable and informative narratives appeared only well after World War II. In 1956 Admiral James published his valuable *The Eyes of the Navy*, in America entitled *The Code Breakers of Room 40*. James also aided David Kahn in his chapter on Room 40 in *The Codebreakers* (1967)[16] and helped me gain access to valuable materials of a similar kind. Fifteen years later Patrick Beesly, an officer in Naval Intelligence during the second war, produced a more thorough study with the title *Room 40: British Naval*

Intelligence 1914-1918. In the interval many documents both British and German had been opened at Kew, and it was possible to make a relatively complete statement. Beesly's main concern was decryption as practised in Room 40 and he therefore devoted only a few pages to the work of divers. Still later, Christopher Andrew produced *Her Majesty's Secret Service* (1986, no mention of "Her Majesty" in the British original edition), with a very thorough and interesting chapter on Room 40, but again with hardly any information on divers. He clearly indicated how much information had become generally available in the last few decades, and listed six volumes of "special telegrams," based on or concerning enemy codes and intercepts, now in the Public Record Office.[17] These volumes contain frequent references to special operations against U-boats but do not confirm the claim by Admiral James that "as soon as the official historians began their work, the secret of the naval [decryption] section had to be divulged because it would have been absurd to invent fictitious stories to explain the movements of the British Fleet in answer to the movements of the German Fleet."[18] In fact, fictitious stories were invented under official auspices, and neither Corbett nor Newbolt seems to have had access to the veridical volumes.

2. Cables and Cable-Cutting

At the beginning of the war both the British and the Germans tried to cut enemy communications transmitted overseas by underwater cables, especially in the Atlantic Ocean. Before the war five telegraph cables passed westward from Emden in the Bight of Heligoland through the Straits of Dover. The two most important, laid in 1900 and 1904, went out to Horta in the Azores and thence across the Atlantic to Coney Island, New York. A third went to Brest in France, a fourth to Vigo in Spain, and yet another to Tenerife in the Canary Islands (thence on to Monrovia, the capital of Liberia, and ultimately to Pernambuco, Brazil). In 1912 the British laid plans for cutting these enemy communication links, and on August 5, 1914, the British cable ship *Telconia* off Emden found and cut all five cables.[19] (Twenty-five years later, at the beginning of World War II, *Cambria* would cut two from Emden to the Azores and Lisbon.[20]) The New York-Azores-Emden cables were diverted during the war, one by the British to Penzance before February 1917,[21] and the other by the French to Brest[22]. By August 1916 the British lifted the cable to Tenerife and re-laid it from Brest to Casablanca[23] and Dakar, thence on to Monrovia[24]. Indeed, as late as November 1918 they were still severing cables in the English Channel. [25]

At the beginning they also made strenuous efforts to cut German communications with Africa. Though the powerful radio station at Nauen, west of Berlin, could transmit as far as Kamina in Togoland, whence messages went by land to Monrovia,[26] both the station at Kamina and the cable from Lome fell into British hands. At midnight on November 19-20, 1914, the Eastern Telegraph Company cut the cable from Monrovia to Tenerife about two hundred miles west of Monrovia and removed thirty miles of it. Later this cable was re-laid from Monrovia to Freetown, Sierra Leone, while "the more northerly sections of this route were used by the French to provide cables from Brest to Casablanca and thence to Dakar." In November and December 1916 the British cable ship *Dacia* was working for the French in order to divert the Emden-Tenerife and Tenerife-Monrovia cables. She was repairing a cable off Casablanca and was to pick up cable off Tenerife, but was sunk by *U38*.[27] A decade later, F. J. Brown wrote that the Monrovia-Pernambuco cable "is still lying derelict at the bottom of the South Atlantic Ocean."[28]

German raiders in the Pacific cut British cables and demolished radio stations. On September 7, 1915, the light cruiser *Nürnberg* wrecked the station on Fanning Island in the central Pacific and cut the cable, while on November 9 the similar raider *Emden* demolished the station on Cocos Island in the Indian Ocean but could not cut the cables before the superintendent sent messages to London and other stations. The Australian light cruiser *Sydney* arrived soon after *Emden's* crew cut the cable to Perth, West Australia, and then sank the German vessel.[29]

U-BOATS AS CABLE-CUTTERS[30]

Wherever a raider appeared there was cause for alarm, even on the American coast. After *U53* attacked shipping off New York in October 1916 the British ambassador Spring Rice informed the Foreign Office "Telegraph Company here fears German submarine will cut cables from Halifax to British Isles, etc."[31] In fact *U53* was not equipped for the task, but the alarm was significant.

From the middle of 1917 the boats used against the Azores and the other islands were chiefly the converted mercantile submarines. First to be rebuilt was *Deutschland* herself, now *U155*, out to the Azores on May 23. On July 4 she shelled the Portuguese port of Ponta Delgada on Sao Miguel, where there was a cable station on the line Lisbon-Horta. On December 12 Gansser in *U156* shelled Funchal, Madeira, in order to damage the cable station there. Other boats tried to cut cables with new grappling devices. In January 1918 Max Valentiner in *U157* tried to cut cables on the rocky bottom off the Azores and, as he had expected, lost the cutting gear.[32] The next month her sister *U155* tried to cut five cables off Lisbon, and a signal made at 1830 on February 13 reported some success. "Appear to have cut cables from Lisbon to Gibraltar [laid in] 1870, both [?to] Madeira [and] San Miguel, Porthcurno 1887 doubtful. Both cable cutters have broken during the operation."[33] The report was almost exact, for three cables were cut: the one from Carcavellos (near Lisbon) to Gibraltar, another to Sao Miguel, a third to

Porthcurno near Falmouth. The two to Madeira, supposedly cut, remained intact. Later ventures off the Azores were not so successful.

CABLES AND NAVIGATION OFF THE FRISIAN ISLANDS

Both the British and the Germans cut cables near the German U-boat routes close to the Frisian Islands. A signal from *U49* at the end of April 1917 revealed an unsuccessful attempt. [34] Presumably she was using a "drag with a special grapnel, with open jaws attached to the submarine's main electric power circuit." The grapnel was intended to "grip the cable, the jaws meet, heat burns through the cable." [35]

Late that summer German cable-cutting trawlers were active near the diving areas along U-boat routes along the Dutch coast. During August they searched for a cable from Fanö in southern Denmark to Calais that ran close to the old Borkum--New York cable and crossed the Yellow Route. They found and cut it on the 14th. On the night of the 15th they were lying at anchor to the northwest of the diving area on the Yellow U-boat route when they sighted British minelayers at work, escorted by destroyers. They might have given warning of a new large minefield but failed to identify the vessels. On September 8 they went out again and cut the northern Fanö-Calais cable about fifty miles north of Terschelling.[36]

Meanwhile the Harwich Force had undertaken fishing of its own. On August 10 destroyers escorted two trawlers out to cut a Borkum--Dover Straits cable just west of Texel. They were recalled because of bad weather, and when they went back on the 14th the trawlers could not find the cables. On the night of August 26 the group went out to the southwest of the U-boat diving area of 018 epsilon VII, where each trawler found a cable and cut it, three and a half miles north 63 east of the Haaks Light Vessel. Five nights later they cut two cables west of Texel and dragged for another, and on September 4 they hooked a cable off Ijmuiden. Both ships cut it and then towed the ends in opposite directions.[37]

On August 30 *U49* was off the West Frisians again, outward bound with orders to cut cables, when she was told by radio that "according to present information one cable Holland-England has been destroyed, probably the southern one." The next afternoon she reported her location, well to the west while fishing for another cable, but on September 3, west of the Dogger Bank, announced that she was heading for the Shetlands because of bad weather and because her cable-cutter was out of order.[38] She did not return from this cruise.

Apparently the Germans were trying not only to cut off communications between Britain, the Netherlands, and Scandinavia but also to prevent interference with the Black and Yellow Routes, while the British were frustrating use of the old cables in the Bight for any purpose.

17

Conceivably the Germans were considering use of the telegraph cables from Emden via Borkum toward the Channel and Brest (and the Azores) for navigating U-boats, since they could not yet rely on the special "navigation cable" or "leader cable", which was to run along the U-boat route out from Borkum.

In July 1917 the Germans regarded their basic Yellow Route out of the Bight of Heligoland as essentially mine-free. Orders issued on July 3 and therefore found in the wreck of *UC44* at the end of September stated that submarines were to follow it whenever possible.[39] The quadrants 010 and 018 epsilon VII, 166 and 167 gamma VII, marked the end of the Yellow Route, 003 epsilon VII the alternative Black Route.

The British gained exact information about these U-boat routes only on August 15 when *E31* returned from scouting near the Terschelling Light Vessel. On the 10th she had discovered buoys marking the beginning of a swept channel and taken sights on them, observing that four trawlers were sweeping mines nearby. She went back to the buoys the next day and dived when she sighted smoke in the distance; after an hour she could make out seven M-class sweepers. Carefully drawn charts and sketches set forth the situation for the Harwich authorities.[40] The three buoys she sighted lay at the north end of the German chart quadrant 018 epsilon VII and just west of 031 epsilon, the diving area for U-boats bound out from German ports.

GERMAN SWEPT CHANNEL BUOYS (YELLOW ROUTE)

```
            0504 0505 0506 0507 0508 0509 0510 0511
5407N       | ----- | ----- | ----- | ----- | ----- | ----- | ----- |
              in 017 e A    |    | 032 e
5406N       | ----- | ----- | ----- | ----- | ----- | ----- | ----- |
                 in 018 e |    | 031 e
5405N       | --B- | ----- | ----- | ----- | ----- | ----- | -C-- |
```

British forces had laid no mines along this route since June 13, but just on the night of August 15-16 minelayers dropped a thousand mines in an irregular pattern in 164 gamma, 012 and 018 epsilon, near buoys A and B, in order to catch U-boats as they dived and headed out to sea. An Admiralty telegram on August 20 asked Harwich for further action. "Their Lordships desire that as soon as you have a submarine ready for minelaying with a full load, you are to send her to lay mines between the buoys reported by *E31*."[41]

MINING THREE U-BOATS

U50 sailed August 30 along the Yellow Route to 010 epsilon, southwest of the buoys observed by *E31*. There she made her last signal, then dived and headed to the northwest. Nothing more was heard from her, and she evidently hit the deep mines British forces had laid on August 15.[43] Next came *U66*, out on September 2 to the Borkum Reef Light Vessel, thence submerged toward the minefield. Spindler writes that she made a signal just after midnight on September 3 from a location near the Dogger Bank and therefore beyond the British mines.[44] The IV U-Boat Flotilla diary places her at 0248 in 157 gamma, NW of the mines in 165 gamma, but British records locate the signal in the equivalent of quadrant 031 epsilon, just east of the diving area and east of the mines she presumably hit.[45] Finally, on the 5th Schwieger took *U88* out from Borkum with *U54* and *U45* under surface escort. That evening he left the escort and submerged ahead of *U54* in 166 gamma, just west of 010 epsilon. All three submarines headed northwest toward the unlocated minefield. An hour later *U54* scraped a mine cable in 012 epsilon and after another hour heard a heavy detonation abaft and above when precisely in 164 gamma. Another, ten minutes later, must have marked the end of *U88*. *U54* tried to radio the news to her base but could not make contact and did not transmit the information before returning to port on October 7. Whatever *U45* heard, she did not report and did not return from her cruise.

THE YELLOW AND BLACK ROUTES[42]

```
          Gamma VII                        Epsilon VII
     0400 0410  0420  0430  0440  0450  0500  0510  0520  0530 0540
5412N------------------------------------------------------------
   | 100 | 125 | 132 | 157 | 164 | 012 | 017 | 032 | 037 | 050 |
5406-------------------------------------------------------------
   | 101 | 124 | 133 | 156 | 165 | 011 | 018 | 031 | 038 | 049 |
5400-------------------------------------------------------------
   | 102 | 123 | 134 | 155 | 166 | 010 | 019 | 030 | 039 | 048 |
5354-------------------------------------------------------------
   | 103 | 122 | 135 | 154 | 167 | 009 | 020 | 029 | 040 | 047 |
5348-------------------------------------------------------------
   | 104 | 121 | 136 | 153 | 168 | 008 | 021 | 028 | 041 | 046 |
5342-------------------------------------------------------------
   | 105 | 120 | 137 | 152 | 169 | 007 | 022 | 027 | 042 | 045 |
5336-------------------------------------------------------------
   | 106 | 119 | 138 | 151 | 170 | 006 | 023 | 026 | 043 | 044 |
5330-------------------------------------------------------------
   | 107 | 118 | 139 | 150 | 001 | 005 | 024 | 025 | Terschelling
5324-------------------------------------------------------------
   | 108 | 117 | 140 | 149 | 002 | 004 | Vlieland & Terschelling
5318---------------------------------------------------------
   | 109 | 116 | 141 | 148 | 003 | Vlieland
5312--0410--0420- 0430--0440--0450
```

19

Obviously the German command was not aware of any of these losses at the time, and the laying of a navigational cable from Borkum, ordered on September 5 but not achieved until the 26th, had nothing to do with the specific locations.[46] Since the cause of the sinkings remained unknown at home as well as abroad, U-boats continued to use the Yellow Route without qualms.

THE CASE OF *U106*

On September 8 the new *U106* under K/L Hufnagel had passed through the minefield on her maiden voyage to the northern North Sea and the Hebrides. The British picked up signals from the diving area in 018 epsilon and, fourteen hours later, near the Dogger Bank. On October 6 she signalled off St. Abbs Head, Scotland, and claimed to have sunk 10,000 tons. She expected to meet an escort the next morning in 018 epsilon at the end of the Yellow Route and just northeast of Quadrant 010. The Admiralty were aware, as a telegram of October 1 stated, that "enemy submarines are using a submerged route east true from 5357N/0405E [102 gamma] as far as longitude 0450E [166 gamma/010 epsilon], thence N56 east true."[47] A watch officer's notebook from *UB81*, sunk December 2, defined the route as precisely from 102 gamma to 010 epsilon.

On September 24 the British had laid 432 new mines a little to the northwest of their earlier field. According to Captain Cowie, these were the first of the new and efficient H2 mines based on German models.[48] Two submarines passed outward through the field the next day. *UB34* struck mine cables at thirty metres and heard explosions in 018 epsilon and 132 gamma, but reported these encounters only after returning home along the same route on the 29th. The other submarine, *UB64*, reported several mine explosions which had caused minor damage but did not answer a signal ordering her to give the exact position. In fact, she supplied it only just before her return on October 19. The Germans therefore had no exact information about the mines.

On the morning of October 7 there was a flurry of German radio activity. Soon after *U106* signalled at 0200 that she was delayed and would arrive on the 8th, not the 7th, the British mines laid in September were discovered. A signal to *U106* ordered her to take the Black Route, which lay toward the south, close to the Frisian Islands. (A paper found by then in *UC44* defines this route as 003 epsilon to 061 epsilon.) Unfortunately she lacked the latest cipher, probably in effect since September 20, and had to reply "Not understood." Four hours later another signal instructed her to enter the Yellow Route only through 167 gamma, the quadrant on a line southwestward from 018 and 010 epsilon. She could not decipher this signal either. No further signals came from the submarine, and escorts sent out to both 018 epsilon and 167 gamma found no trace of her.

She may have struck one of the mines laid in September, but perhaps E51 was directly responsible for her demise. This submarine left Harwich at 0530 on October 6, several hours after U106 announced her destination, and laid twenty mines to the southwest of that point. Admiralty records indicate that the location, in approximately 010 epsilon[49], was forty miles north of Vlieland "on the [Yellow] route which was the most used at that time." E51 was preventing access to 018 epsilon by mining 010, just southwest of it. On the 10th E34 laid more mines still farther to the southwest.

The BdU (Commanding Officer U-Boats) and the Admiralty Staff found the losses alarming. A memorandum on the afternoon of October 9 stated that deep mines and nets, apparently linked together, lay on the extension of the Yellow Route. U50 had certainly been lost on it, since on September 23 her commander's corpse had come ashore on a North Frisian beach south of Sylt. Probably U88 and possibly U106 and UC42 had disappeared for the same reason. The southern routes in the Bight were no longer safe. A BdU signal the next day gave U-boats this information, and on the 10th a British Admiralty telegram noted that they had begun to pass in and out through the Skagerrak.[50] Evidently the new cable, intended to guide them, had achieved little or nothing.

THE MINING OF UB61 AND U75

In November E51 struck against the Black Route, laying mines in 004 epsilon off Vlieland on the 18th and the 23rd. Her report on the 25th gives the location on the 23rd as "not the line actually aimed at, but ...as near as the circumstances and weather allowed." The twenty mines were only eight feet beneath the surface. Signals intercepted on the 29th revealed success. Late that evening UB61 and a trawler struck mines and sank after heavy seas had kept escorts from sweeping. The trawler left nine survivors, the U-boat none. The location was given inexactly as 001 epsilon.

The Black Route was immediately closed, and all U-boats in the Bight took the Yellow Route, now swept again. German signals made this plain, as did the notebook taken from a survivor of UB81. Still farther east, therefore, E51 dropped twenty more mines on December 12. A signal the next morning showed that U75 was proceeding out on this route, but that evening another signal revealed that she had blown up in the field. There were nine survivors. The situation was rather confused at the time, and the precise location may not have been the one found in the German records but about 5357N/0537E (048 epsilon), where the mines were laid and a minesweeper was sunk on December 28.[51] Gladisch comments that "the field lay exactly on the route, and it is certainly possible that E51 watched the escorts and then deposited the field." More probably her information came from radio and the notebook. Apart from *UB22*, sunk on the route toward Horns Reef in January 1918, this was the last sinking along the U-boat routes in the Bight. More constant and careful sweeping and escorting prevented any further losses.

ROUTES AND CABLES NEAR ZEEBRUGGE

On August 5 the Flanders command realized that because of mines it was necessary to sweep five entrance/exit routes near Zeebrugge and not let them be noted in log books. The first, called Route 2501, led in from a Fairy Bank lattice-work buoy bearing that number to the Zeebrugge Mole. Routes 3 and 4 provided ways to get in from the Schouwen Bank Light Vessel. The most sophisticated were Routes A and B, out from Zeebrugge to the northwest and the north, each provided with a "navigation cable" signalling "AT" for "Anton" and "BE" for "Berta." When Gibson and Prendergast say a leader cable was laid "along the Thornton Ridge" a year later[52] they are referring to Route B.

MINING OF *UC21*, *UC14*, AND *UC16*

The new system could not have prevented three mine-related sinkings in late September and October. First, *UC21* went out September 13 for the French west coast and was due back within a fortnight. In the interval the British destroyer *Meteor* had laid two fields totalling eighty mines in quadrants 036 and 037 beta, north of Zeebrugge, and coastal motor boats had deposited five more in 062 beta. None of these mines were found before *UC21* returned and quite possibly encountered what *Meteor* had laid. Next was the small *UC14*, out October 1 to lay mines later found in the Stanford Channel off Yarmouth. On the evening of the 3rd, shore stations at Zeebrugge and Knocke observed a bright flash and a violent explosion to the north of Zeebrugge. Evidently *UC14* had hit one of the mines laid by the motor boats. Finally, *UC16* left Zeebrugge on October 2 and probably laid her mines off Boulogne a few days later. One of the new fields must have accounted for her, since the corpse of her watch officer was found October 26 at Noordwijk on the Dutch coast. Mines thus accounted for three boats in less than a fortnight. Thereafter, however, no U-boat hit mines off the Belgian coast, though British minefields had continued to grow during the spring and summer of 1917, and Robinson tells how Zeppelins looked for mines to the west of those already sighted in quadrants 037 and 038 epsilon.[53]

ROUTES IN 1918

During 1918 the British closely listened to radio signals on the submarine routes close to the Flanders coast. These revealed that from January through March U-boat commanders favoured Routes A and B, while they generally employed Route B to Thornton Ridge off Wenduyne in April and May. U-boats heading homeward made signals from quadrants 031 and 007 beta.

At the end of May British minelayers planted a large field along Route B north of Thornton Ridge and in the direction of North Hinder (037 beta). Signals intelligence could follow events with some ease after *UC64*, inward bound on Route B the next morning, was told to stop because of danger, then informed that a mine had been found in quadrant 037 beta. Orders would be sent later -- in fact ten hours later, when both *UB30* and *UC64* were ordered to come in from quadrant 032 beta "along Route 3."

Early in June a prisoner from *UC75* stated that the boat "generally followed 'Route A' which appears to lead roughly true West for three or four miles."[54] In fact, however, Route 3 was used to a greater extent in June and July, with locations equivalent to 808K and 859K, and because of constant sweeping remained safe until early August. What was needed, however, was a way to the west, and on June 28 Route A, about a mile wide, was finally opened up.

K-QUADRANTS (=original beta VI) NORTH AND WEST OF ZEEBRUGGE

```
LONG--0230E  0240   0250   0300   0310   0320   0330
5154N   -----------------------------------------------
       | 1059 | 1009 |  959 |  909 |  859 |  809 |
       |      |      |      |      | =001 | =002 |
5148    -----------------------------------------------
       | 1058 | 1008 |  958 |  908 |  858 |  808 |
       | =011 | =010 | =009 | =008 | =007 | =006 |
5142    ------------------------------------------------
       | 1057 | 1007 |  957 |  907 |  857 |  807 |Schelde
       | =028 | =029 | =030 | =031 | =032 | =033 | =034
5136    ------------------------------------------------
       | 1056 | 1006 |  956 |  906 |  856 |  806 |
       | =040 | =039 | =038 | =037 | =036 | =035|
5130    ------------------------------------------
       | 1055 | 1005 |  955 |  905 |  855 |
       | =058 | =059 | =060 | =061 | =062 |
5124    ----------------------------------------
       | 1054 | 1004 |  954 |  904 | Zeebrugge
       | =066 | =065 | =064 | =063 |
  5118  ------------------ Ostend----Wenduyne
```

A memorandum sent Captain James in late September 1918 -- just after the U-boats had left Flanders -- points to decryption difficulties.[55] "The

23

tracing of these [routes] is hampered by the fact that messages in June and July, when Route 3 was in use, have not yet been decoded, and the August messages only partially so." On the other hand, enough was read so that the memorandum could define five routes. The first was Route B, with "gathering squares" in 907K (030 beta) and 858 (008 beta). It was defined by a signal made to WHK [WHQ, UC64] and ran between Raabs Bank and the Thornton Ridge on Wenduyne, "turning off when the Mole bears about 110 degrees." Route 3 had gathering squares in 808 (old 007) and 859 (old 170). It apparently led at about 186 degrees from the point on the Middle Bank where several tracks met, and to Zeebrugge between Schooneveld and Raan Banks. Route A, almost the only route used in September and August, included a rendezvous for torpedo-boat escorts in the middle of 955K (060 beta), thence probably leading directly to Zeebrugge. (Since Route 4 was hardly ever mentioned it did not need to be plotted.) This much knowledge about routes meant that returning U-boats might be attacked, though not in locations that might give away the efficiency of decryption.

M-SINKERS

The routes in to Zeebrugge were further complicated on the night of August 7-8, when British destroyers laid a field of 234 new magnetic mines about eight miles to the north of Zeebrugge, close to the end of Route B. (Unfortunately, U-boats were now taking Route A.) These mines, called "M destructors" or "M-sinkers," did not have cables but simply dropped to the bottom, where they were set off magnetically by passing steel ships.[56] Hartmann says they were detonated by a "two-needle magnetic mechanism and acoustic chattering relay,"[57] or as Admiral Ruge puts it more simply, they worked on the principle of the compass.[58] Roger Keyes, commanding at Dover, was pleased with the operation, "successfully carried out without any interference by the enemy, and apparently entirely unobserved by them." That afternoon the German destroyer V68 was sunk by a mine in 855K, exactly on Route B in the Schooneveld Bank, and on the 11th G41 was slightly damaged. Keyes tells how eagerly the British listened for news of results. "From air reconnaissance and other reports, we knew that a German destroyer had been sunk in it the following morning; other explosions had been located in the minefield by our directional station, which we hoped were the minesweepers, sent out to sweep up our minefield, blowing up."[59] (Fortunately for UB111, out from Zeebrugge at 0205 on the 11th, she took Route 3 and encountered no mines.[60]) On the 15th the torpedo boat A58, mined in 855K, sank off Zeebrugge, and the trawler Frigg sank the next day.[61] German sweepers were unable to find the mines because they were hemispherical in shape and lay flat on the bottom. Evidently they were ground mines, set off either by magnets or sound devices. Ruge notes that detonations twenty or thirty metres away from torpedo-boats soon betrayed the principle involved, and no U-boats were sunk or damaged.

THE DIFFICULTIES OF UC71

A few days later two U-boats trying to reach Zeebrugge illustrated what Hall liked to call "difficulties." On the morning of August 13 *UC71* under Warzecha tried to get through the Folkestone Gate but was damaged by shore-controlled mines and spent most of the day on the surface, driving hostile airplanes away with shrapnel. Her signals were read with interest by both sides. At 0935 she stated that she had hit a mine in the Channel and could not dive. Since she was now in 1105K, north of Dunkirk, she was ordered to proceed to 1007K, off Thornton Ridge, where five German planes would give protection. The British were unable to decipher her speed and location or the position to which she was being ordered, since Bruges was using a new chart. At the morning briefing in London Sims was told simply, "a Flanders submarine reports that she struck a mine in the Channel and was badly damaged." Around that time a plane from Dunkirk found her and dropped two bombs, which forced her to dive. Later she surfaced and drove other planes away with gunfire. Tests had shown there were no magnetic mines on Route A, the route she followed to Zeebrugge that afternoon.

THE MYSTERY OF UB57

Early on the afternoon of August 14 *UB57* under Lohs was the only U-boat in the Straits of Dover, and she must have been the submarine sighted on the surface off Gris Nez by a British seaplane. She was crossing the barrage homeward-bound after Bruges radio warned about the mines just encountered off Folkestone by *UC71*, but she had not come close enough to the French coast to be heard by the coastal hydrophones. Between 1800 and 1900 hours, however, patrols out from Dunkirk used their hydrophones to follow a submerged submarine nine miles north of Calais and slightly to the east. They dropped twenty-four depth charges in the vicinity, between the Sandettie and Outer Ruytingen Shoals. After 1900 the submarine's motors were still faintly audible "in a zone where pursuit was not possible," because of shoal waters or mines. At 2100 a plane or a patrol reported a submarine making for the northeast, twenty miles north of Gravelines.

UB57 made a signal to Bruges at 2250 German time and it was immediately read at home and abroad. "Have sunk three steamers, fifteen thousand tons, entering Route A," northwest of Zeebrugge along a leader cable. Almost at once five coastal motorboats proceeded out from Dunkirk toward Ostend. Their speed was about three times that of the U-boat, and they might have cut her off had not bad weather forced them to return at 0130 on the 15th.

The signal from *UB57* lacked important information. She did not give her position, for enemy forces were not far away. Triangulation by both the British and the Germans showed that she was close to the eastern end of the Sandettie Bank. More important, she did not say when she would arrive in Zeebrugge. Bruges asked about the time in a signal made at 2340, but there was no answer. Perhaps the U-boat had gone to the bottom for the night or experienced some difficulty. In any case nothing more was heard and no one knows what happened to her. If she continued on she should have reached the beginning of Route A no later than 0300, since the distance from Sandettie Bank to the entry point was about twenty miles.

UB103 left Zeebrugge at 2255 on the night of August 14 and probably followed Route A outward (she did not return from her cruise), reaching the end by 0200 and then heading west.[62] To judge from the times when *UB57* made her signal (2250) and *UB103* should have entered or left Route A (0200, 0315), one would expect some contact between the two. Since none was made or, at any rate, reported, she may have sunk before reaching it. Since both submarines were sunk, however, precision is impossible.

Further information makes the situation even more obscure. On September 1 the corpse of a machinist's mate from *UB57* was found on the beach at Den Haan near Wenduyne, and a week later an autopsy revealed a bullet wound in the head. What can have caused it? Neither French nor British records report any activity by patrols or aircraft during the night that could explain the situation, though conceivably aircraft subsequently shot down or simply missing were responsible. The shooting deepens the mystery of the loss.

A British chart once on display in the Submarine Museum at Zeebrugge placed the wreck of *UB57* only two miles north of Zeebrugge, and other bodies washed ashore support some such location. Corpses including those of Lohs, her commander, and a chief boatswain's mate came ashore near Flushing, Holland, fifteen miles east of Zeebrugge, on August 22, while on September 2 the body of a sailor was found at Ostend and that of the watch officer at Zeebrugge. Coastal currents may explain the distribution, though the compiler of the list of lost U-boats in the fifth volume of *Der Handelskrieg mit U-Booten* may have known or surmised that after Lohs abandoned ship the watch officer took command. For whatever reason, he lists the watch officer as the commander of the lost submarine.[63]

THE LEADER CABLES

We do not know whether or not *UB57* intended to follow the leader cable along Route A, though it certainly existed. In May 1918 talkative survivors from *UB85* had discussed the "future" fitting of hinged rectangular frames just before the conning tower (one horizontal, one vertical), "each carrying about fifty turns of insulated wire." A current would be induced when the boat approached an electric cable lying on the bottom, for example out of Borkum. The boat would approach zig-zag, and when it was over the cable the letters being signalled on it would be at their loudest. The Admiralty Experimental Station thought that the international telegraph cables cut early in the war were being used for this purpose. Two weeks later the Director of the Anti-Submarine Division proposed to equip a Harwich submarine to detect the seaward ends of the cables and then patrol near them. By June 11 a submarine from the South Dogger Bank Patrol was to be sent out. The file contains no further mention of the scheme, however, and perhaps the plan was scrapped as more information came in.[64] At the daily briefing on May 21 it was announced that the leader cables had been "ascertained." The navigation apparatus was mentioned by prisoners taken between April and August from no fewer than five U-boats, three from Flanders and two from the Bight of Heligoland.[65] The interrogators seem to have been fishing for information when they got answers about the cable, and they were rather surprised, as was Hall himself, at what they discovered. All the prisoners insisted that in any event their own boats did not carry the equipment, and Schmitz of *UC75* insisted that he was "quite able to find his way without it."

BYWATER ON FLANDERS CABLES
H. C. Bywater tells a dramatic tale of revelations made by a U-boat officer fearful of being turned over to "a certain Allied government" for an atrocity. This officer talked so freely about the "leader gear" that "there is reason to believe that a week or so later the Zeebrugge-Ostend leader cables suddenly ceased to function, with the result that certain U-boats homeward bound lost their bearings at a critical moment, blundered into a minefield or nets, and were no more seen."[66] As it stands, the story is not reliable. The prisoner in question is modelled upon Robert Moraht, captured from *U64* on June 17, who was sought by the French and was told about their interest in him.[67] There is no reason, however, to suppose he knew details about cables off Flanders.[68] The only submarine that could have been sunk under these circumstances in the period after Moraht's capture was *UB57*, but as we have seen no one knows just how she was lost.

THE CABLES IN SEPTEMBER 1918
British divers do not seem to have found U-boats equipped with the metal frames that were described in May, though papers recovered from *UB109* early in September might have mentioned the cables. Late that month a prisoner from that submarine stated that a leader cable used for U-boat transits off Zeebrugge ran from "the red conical buoy at the northern end of Thornton Ridge towards Wenduyne Church" (the latter being south of Quadrant 063 on our chart). He was describing Route B, no longer in use.

Interrogators regarded him as "generally reliable," but Hall noted that "there is no other evidence tending either to confirm or disprove the above."[69] The prisoner also inconsistently claimed that since Flanders submarines were not equipped with the "navigation apparatus," only destroyers and torpedo boats used it "for passing in or out of Zeebrugge during thick weather." It appears that the British knew nothing about cable locations off Zeebrugge, even though the device may have been partly responsible for the safety of U-boats off the Flanders coast during 1918. Bywater's claim may thus contain elements of truth.

The news from *UB109* was sent to British authorities at Zeebrugge after the port had been captured. At that time an officer said he had seen the buoy near Thornton Ridge. "The buoy is probably gone by now, but the cable remains undoubtedly."

Too late for any practical use, the Admiralty obtained a highly valuable document from the First Section of the French General Staff. (It is to be found at the very end of the Dover records.) It is not dated, but perhaps was obtained after the fall of Zeebrugge. It is important because it contains the "navigation orders for the Belgian coast," definitely on board such U-boats entered by divers as *UB109* and *UC70*.[70] The tenth paragraph reads as follows:

> Two navigation cables go out from Wenduyne to facilitate making land on the Flanders coast. The first goes out from Wenduyne and extends three miles to the north, then is oriented at 290 degrees to the middle of quadrant 059 beta. The second goes out from Wenduyne and is oriented at 355 degrees until it reaches the parallel 51 degrees 35 minutes north.

This exact information reached London too late to be of any use. Even if it was also found in *UB109*, the U-boats were about to abandon the Straits route, and they left Flanders for good at the end of September. To be sure, coastal motor boats laid a few mines near Wenduyne on September 20, perhaps relying on information about cables, but there was no result.

3. Divers and Searchers

When U-boats at sea made signals their locations could be checked by "radiogoniometry," but reading the signals was more important. Information from prisoners, signals, and wrecks was valuable, especially when coordinated in the Naval Intelligence Department. Roskill gave high praise to the director. "In a conflict from which the Admiralty does not in general emerge well Hall's work was the outstanding exception."[71] His brilliant and idiosyncratic conduct of the Department brought remarkable results, summarized in the biography by his sometime assistant "Bubbles" James.[72] A few of his own notes are preserved in the archives of Churchill College, Cambridge, while many documents in the Admiralty files contain comments and directives. Part of his daily routine is also known from briefings given Admiral Sims or a representative in London each morning from the end of 1917 onwards. Summaries of these are to be found in the National Archives in Washington.

INTERCEPTION OF RADIO COMMUNICATIONS

Radio communications played a novel and important part in the naval war. The first British patents of Guglielmo Marconi for wireless telegraphy (radio) dated only from 1896, but the marine use and development of systems had been rapid. The Germans used Marconi's apparatus from 1897 onward and three years later built a station on the island of Borkum. By the outbreak of the war all naval vessels of any importance, including submarines, made use of radio. Because of possible interception, the first U-boat foray began with radio silence maintained.[73] In general, however, U-boats exchanged signals with Nauen, Norddeich, and Neumünster in Germany, as well as the light cruiser *Arcona* in the Ems estuary and the steamer *Rugia*, especially equipped to receive and transmit. Very early, and throughout the war, U-boats tried to set records for long-distance transmission and reception. Frank Birch of Room 40 suggests that the Germans neglected the likelihood of interception because they did not know how wide the range of their wireless was.[74] He also tells how "in 1917 the sending of W. T. signals on a very low wave length, ranging from 180 to 200 metres, was inaugurated and so sure were the authorities that it could not possibly be intercepted by English stations that 'en clair' messages were sent by this method."[75] Hall told Sims about such 'en clair' messages in January 1918.

The British had been listening to German radio since the beginning of the war, when they had to decide whether to jam the traffic or try to read it. When they proceeded to intercept, a new era of decoding and decryption was inaugurated. They also developed the use of radio direction finding and gradually established a network of shore stations for this purpose and for interception as well. British and French decryption of signals brought almost up-to-date information about U-boat activities. From time to time, because of atmospheric conditions or the weakness of signals, stations on the British coast could pick up U-boat messages not received at home.

BRITISH DIRECTION FINDING

At the beginning of the war both British and Germans were busy with direction finding or radiogoniometry, the measurement of angles of reception. Maurice Wright, the Marconi Engineer in Chief, worked on detecting radio signals. As the Marconi station at Chelmsford started picking up German naval signals on July 30, 1914, they were taken to a friend of Hall, who (it is said) "arranged for Wright to travel up to Liverpool Street on the footplate of a specially chartered locomotive." Hall then had naval stations built for intercepting signals and finding directions. Eventually Wright was able to differentiate a useful signal and its bearing from other interfering signals. Early in 1915, he set up a direction-finding radio in Christiania (now Oslo), Norway, and successfully ran it for several months. When he saw a poster for his arrest, however, he left for the southwest coast and was picked up by a destroyer. Many years later his son, the author of *Spycatcher*, tried to find details of this operation in the MI6 files. He says he was allowed to spend a day at their registry, but he concluded that "the MI6 weeders had routinely destroyed all the records years before."[76]

James and Beesly also ascribe the foundation to the Marconi Company and tell how the receiving station was moved to Lowestoft, while others were established at Lerwick, Aberdeen, York, Flamborough Head, and Birchington. Some were used to record signals as well as locate them. Eventually there were fourteen in all, and they produced a constant flow of reports about U-boat signals and their contents, all transmitted to London for correlation and, ultimately, decryption.[77]

Patrick Beesly discusses the accuracy of the fixes when grid quadrants were not deciphered, claiming that in 1917 "Direction Finding, whatever its degree of accuracy, often gave the swiftest clue to the position of a U-boat." On the other hand, "based on World War II experience, it is unlikely that fixes were accurate to within a smaller radius than twenty miles from a central point even in the North Sea, while in the more distant areas, out in the Atlantic, a fifty mile radius was probably the best that could be given."[78] Other estimates agree with his conclusion,[79] and indeed the British fixed most of the U-boat positions by deciphering the signals.

GERMAN DIRECTION FINDING

In 1915 "the first German direction-finding stations were being completed at Nordholz [near Cuxhaven] and [the Frisian island of] Borkum to serve the Naval Airship Division. At first the airship called up the shore station, which measured the direction of her signals and radioed the bearings to the Zeppelin, where they were plotted on a chart." The procedure was first used by *L9* on April 19, 1915. Three months later a Zeppelin tried to use radio bearings over England, but the attempt failed because "the two direction-finding stations at Borkum and Nordholz were nearly in line with *L10's* position over the Northumberland coast." Other stations were later added at List on Sylt and at Bruges, but difficulties remained. A Zeppelin taking part in a raid in October 1917 noted that "bearings could not be obtained; all the ships were calling."[80]

In his biography of his father, A. W. Ewing notes that when a Zeppelin over the North Sea made a signal so that the German directional stations could tell it where it was, British directional stations found that the positions usually "agreed well" with their own calculations.[81]

Robinson explains the new method employed at the end of 1917 when the radio direction-finding organization was redesigned.

Two new sending stations were erected at Tondern [Zeppelin base in Schleswig, now Toender in Denmark] and at Cleve, 250 miles to the south-south-west in the Rhineland [just east of Nijmegen, Holland]. These transmitted directional signals on a regular schedule, fifteen minutes before and fifteen minutes after the hour, and an airship could determine her bearing from each station with her own radio receiver and the long trailing antenna, using no special equipment except a stop-watch and great circle charts.[82]

Nevertheless, on March 12 there were "errors in the radio bearings" and again on August 5.[83]

Dr. Walle reveals that this method was not used by Zeppelins alone.

In 1917 the possibility of an electronic locator for the U-boats was important on navigational grounds. In 1917 rotating transmitters were erected in Cleve and Tondern. With the aid of these electronic aids to navigation, even in poor visibility U-boats could determine their positions accurately, which was important for avoiding their own minefields in the North Sea and known enemy ones. Next to the radio activity also conducted by the other coastal radio stations, these rotating transmitters were the first of the permanent installations for electronic navigation that were to be erected [after the war] for merchant shipping and air transport.

He reports that in February 1918 *UB77* while off the west coast of Scotland and near the North Channel could get usable electronic positions from the transmitters at Cleve and Tondern [84] -- though the primary purpose of the transmissions was to help Zeppelins reach Liverpool, a goal never achieved.[85]

(In 1940 German bombers relied on "Knickebein" radio waves from Cleve and Bredstedt [-Husum in Schleswig], as well as "X-beams" from other stations. British scientists do not seem to have recalled the Zeppelin methods of 1915-1918, though conceivably "Cleve" could have rung a bell. The west of England was out of range, as in 1918.)[86]

SECRETS FROM THE SKY AND THE DEEP

The British always needed fresh information from the sky or the bottom of the sea, and a surprising source of U-boat intelligence was found in the wrecks of German Zeppelins, under naval command and therefore using naval codes and ciphers. It was important to investigate the twisted girders that might be left around a control car when the Zeppelin crashed on land or in shallow water. Such wreckage provided more than a few finds.

Comparable materials were available in the wrecks of U-boats sunk in coastal waters, where divers discovered about twenty-five of them, with richer or poorer rewards in ten cases. Much depended on chance. Twenty years after the war Hall claimed he gave standing orders for divers "to open torpedo-hatch, open five water-tight doors, turn sharp to right and retrieve top drawer in which were all papers."[87] Few submarines could be entered so easily, however. In fact he was recalling the successful entry into *UB109* in September 1918, not some ordinary procedure.[88] At times, indeed, conning towers had to be blown off to gain access to control rooms.

Divers did not go down simply to obtain secret papers, though Hall laid special emphasis on this goal, but also to assess the nature and extent of the damage suffered by the U-boat, and recover periscopes, guns, ammunition, torpedoes with various kinds of pistols, and even mines. It was important to identify the wreck, though this was not always possible before British and German records were correlated after the war, sometimes not even then. Beesly notes that many UC-boats were visited because these minelayers worked in shallow coastal waters. "Most of the considerable haul of secret papers recovered during the second half of 1917 and in 1918 came from this class of boat."[89] In addition, the UC-boats had a mysterious tendency to blow up while laying mines. The first wreck to be investigated by divers was *UC2*, blown up by her own mine in 1915. Another was *UC12*, similarly sunk and then raised off Taranto in 1916. During 1917 one UC-boat was damaged by its own mine (*UC33* on February 13[90]) and five were sunk in this way: *UC32* on February 23, *UC76* on May 10,[91] *UC44* on August 4, *UC41* on August 21, and *UC42* in September. No such sinkings occurred thereafter, however.

Often divers got into wrecks too late to obtain useful information or, indeed, any information at all. The ten submarines from which British divers took "special materials" were therefore highly significant,[92] not to mention *UC12* raised by the Italians and *UB26* by the French, as well as *UC61*, stranded near Gris Nez and searched by the French.

We should not imagine that the Allies were the only retrievers of documents. After the British submarine *E3* was torpedoed by *U27* south of the Borkum Light Vessel in October, 1914, the naval attaché in Paris suggested to the Admiralty that "the Germans having raised submarine *E3*, it is very probable that they have got possession of our code."[93] When *E15* ran aground in the Dardanelles under the guns of Fort Dardanus on May 16, 1915, British forces made strenuous efforts to blow up the wreck. Lorey says the Turks recovered nothing but pieces of a torpedo, but in fact they obtained papers locating minefields in the Channel and the North Sea and listing British call signs. These papers were sent on to the German Baltic command and thence to the radio station at Neumünster.[94]

On September 4 the British *E7* got caught in a net off Fort Nagara and was still trying to get free at forty metres when von Heimburg, passing by in *UB14*, supplied explosives which a diver attached to the hull. The leaking submarine was able to surface before sinking, and her complement was rescued. [95] Presumably documents could be recovered.

Again, at the end of October the French submarine *Turquoise* patrolled for a week in the Sea of Marmara along with the British *E12, E20*, and *H1*, but homeward-bound on the 30th she ran aground just north of the Dardanelles and surfaced under the guns of a Turkish battery. After her captain surrendered and abandoned ship, a Turkish boarding party recovered her confidential papers (at four metres) and von Heimburg received orders to sail at once from Constantinople with *UB14*.

> According to information from *Turquoise*, presence of *E12, E20*, and *H1* in Sea of Marmara probable. Rendezvous of enemy submarines between 0900 and 1000 and 1600 and 1700 in 2810/4045N...Operation: *UB14* to sail at midnight November 4 and to be escorted out of the Bosporus by a gunboat. Transport of *Turquoise* from Palatia to Constantinople to be expected November 5.

At 1600 on the 5th *UB14* was waiting submerged at the rendezvous when Heimburg sighted an enemy conning tower. An hour and a quarter later he hit the submarine with one torpedo, then surfaced to pick up two officers and six men. *E20* had been due home shortly, and there were no further sinkings of this kind.[96] According to Birch, Heimburg himself had arranged the rendezvous by radioing *E20* in British cipher.[97]

Eighty years later the Australian ambassador to Turkey asked Selcuk Kolay, director of the Rahmi Koc Museum in Istanbul, to search for the wreck of the submarine *AE2*, damaged by shore batteries near the Bosporus on April 30, 1915, and then scuttled. Selcuk Kolay dived on to her on July 2, 1998. He also found the wreck of *UB46*, mined nearby on December 7, 1916.[98]

4.   Codes, Ciphers and Call Signs

THE *MAGDEBURG* CODEBOOK
By April 1915 the British had captured all three of the basic German codebooks.   An important factor in British success was the famous

Magdeburg book, a naval codebook which the Russians acquired and sent to London in mid-October, 1914.[99] When the German "small cruiser" *Magdeburg* ran aground in fog while scouting the entrance to the Gulf of Finland two Russian cruisers came up and opened fire before confidential papers could be destroyed. In the subsequent confusion the Russians obtained "the codebook, the current key, a copy of the German naval gridded chart for the Baltic, the bridge log and the ship's War Diary."

Winston Churchill later told a romantic story of how the petty officer assigned to destroy the code book was killed with the book wired to his body -- soon recovered by the Russians. Beesly more soberly remarked that the book at Kew "shows no signs of immersion in the salt waters of the Baltic."[100] My own observation confirms his point, and indeed this copy is stamped *Kaiserliche Marine. Commando der Nordseestation.* Since several passages are marked "This note is not in 1st copy," the book in this file at Kew is not the original *Magdeburg* book. Mäkelä clears up the mystery. The book at Kew is one of the three *Magdeburg* books, not one, which the Russians acquired. Two were found on the bottom near the wreck, while the third, evidently left on board the cruiser, is No. 151 in the Record Office.[101] This is the one the Russians offered to the Admiralty, and after transport from a port near Murmansk it was delivered to Churchill, the First Lord, on October 13. Conceivably it was used for reading German naval signals a week or so later. It was the basic naval codebook, the *Signalbuch der Kaiserlichen Marine* or *SKM*, in use until May 1917.[102]

The Commander in Chief of the Home Fleet had heard about the book on November 9, when he asked the Admiralty for "signal books, ciphers, position squares etc brought by Captain Kedroff" from Russia. A month later he simply asked for the code. Ten days after that he asked again and Churchill noted on his request, "Surely he ought not to talk about this in this open way... It looks most reckless." Admiral Oliver, then Director of the Intelligence Division, commented, "It does not augur well for the secrecy which will obtain when he gets the books."[103] Eventually he did get them, however.

OTHER CODEBOOKS

The British obtained other important codebooks early in the war.[104] There was the *Handelschiffsverkehrsbuch* (HVB), the *Commercial Substitution Book* used by U-boats and Zeppelins with a 3-letter cipher until March 21, 1915,[105] British and French cryptographers actively investigated it and its encipherments, and in the autumn of 1915 the French were already reading it regularly.[106] Though the Germans knew it had fallen into British hands, they replaced it with AFB only on March 16, 1916, and the British were soon able to obtain copies, one from the Zeppelin *L32*, others from U-boat wrecks.[107] Finally, there was the *Substitution Book* or VB, discovered by chance near the wreck of the German destroyer *S119* off the Dutch coast on November 30, 1914, and brought to London three days later.[108]

CIPHERS, ETC.

Certainly the Germans were aware of French and British investigations into débris from Zeppelins. Indeed, French radio picked up an erroneous German signal that said the wreck of *L19*, down in the North Sea on February 2, 1916, had been picked up by the British and would be examined by French engineers. [109] On February 21 an incendiary shell hit the Army Zeppelin *LZ77* over France,[110] and burned fragments of the HVB code book, in use from January 1 to March 16, were found in the wreck the next day.[111] Secrecy was obviously important, but the journal *La Liberté* reported that "from documents found on board, the dirigible would be the *LZ77*." The Army published a denial at once, but mischief may have been done already. Within five weeks the French copied the dictionary and restored missing sections, but on March 16 HVB was replaced by FVB, *Radio Substitution Book*, possibly but not certainly because of the news.[112]

In northern waters the U-boats began using a 4-letter cipher at noon on March 15 and continued doing so until July 1. This cipher was worked out in Room 40, though our authorities disagree as to what it was. Givierge calls it FVB, though Beesly says it was AFB (General Radio Book).[113] There is some confusion in accounts of cipher changes in 1916 and early 1917, but it appears that at first the cipher Gamma Epsilon was modified on February 10, March 11, April 2 and 11, and May 1,[114] then changed daily from early May.[115] Gamma Upsilon, employed in a signal of February 23, was changed twice a month until May 30, then every Monday.[116]

The cipher system in use from July 1 to December 10 was worked out in Room 40 as in Paris. On July 27, says Givierge, the Section du Chiffre in Paris could read the 3-letter naval code FFB (*Fleet Radio Book*) as well as the 4-letter AFB, with double enciphering frequently changed, and the VB code used by the German naval attaché in Madrid (*Substitution Book*).[117] The British were aware of a "big change" on July 27,[118] and on August 8 an order from the BdU to High Seas Fleet U-boats instructed them to carry SKM plus FVB and Gamma Upsilon and Gamma Alpha ciphers plus Gamma Lambda 3 for the High Seas Fleet. On September 24, however, the wreckage of the Zeppelin *L32* yielded the new AFB, *General Radio Book*, which according to Beesly had entered service early in the year.[119] The wreck of *L33*, downed the same day, yielded the *Weather Key* and the Zeppelin's radio log book up to September 23. The last entry, at 10:58, was "from DK to OK, signed KK."[120] In addition, the intact airship "provided the Admiralty with the latest German operational concepts" and also "indicated how miserably far behind the British designs were."[121] (For the losses of these two Zeppelins see Chapter 5)

A note by Captain Hope of ID 25 illustrates the difficulties encountered that November. "There have been quite a number of messages [from Nauen] commencing with three different kind of symbols:- 'Gamma plus' 'Gamma epsilon' and Gamma gamma.' This series of messages all bear a certain resemblance to each other, and none of them look as though they were based on any of the signal books which we have." On the 17th, however, "a message was sent out from Nauen commencing 'Gamma O.'" Unlike the others, this cipher "does have the appearance of being based on the signal books," and "it is laid down in the Signal Book that 'Gamma O' is the sign of the secret cipher of the Higher Command."[122] Further investigation was obviously needed.

AFB, apparently in use from December 10, 1916, to May 1, 1917, was found again in the wreckage of the Zeppelin *L39*, shot down on March 17, and photographs of the codebook were sent to the French cryptographic section in June, but nothing much was done with them.[123] The Germans learned about the Zeppelin's destruction from an Eiffel Tower news broadcast.[124]

On May 1, 1917, FVB was definitely withdrawn and replaced by AFB.[125] AFB itself was altered on May 31 and was to be changed on the 20th of June, August, and September, October 23, November 25, 1917, and January 20, 1918.[126] On June 17 the wreck of *L48* yielded a "general cipher table for the naval signal book" plus three lists of code words. Admiral Scheer was aware that the British might have recovered such information, since the Zeppelin had been lost over Theberton, Suffolk, and five days later he requested the change of all ciphers.[127] (AFB must have been changed already and "U-cruisers" continued to use Gamma Epsilon.[128]) On June 30 Captain Hope admitted that the homeward-bound *U94* and *U50* had been "communicating pretty freely with each other but we cannot make out what they are saying." The situation gradually improved, however.[129] Documents recovered on September 29 after the wreck of *UC44* was salved included AFB as issued on February 1, 1917, with alterations made on various dates, and the list of call signs for May 1.[130] The codebook bears the title "Radio Substitution Book (F. V. B.), Plan for 1916," but a British correction states, "For F. V. B. read A. F. B." (see above).

On September 19 an Admiralty telegram to coastal commands summed up procedures followed in the case of *UC44*.

Whenever a German submarine is salved all papers, books and documents are to be carefully collected and sent by hand of an officer direct to Director of Intelligence, Admiralty. Utmost secrecy should be maintained regarding this. Bodies should be searched and all papers on them sent up separately to same address. It is important to ascertain names of ranks and ratings. Burial of bodies should take place at sea.

The style points to Hall as the author of the order, though he certainly did not suppose that U-boats were frequently salved. At Dover Bacon reiterated part of it on December 20 when he ordered the Captain of the Dover Patrol to "keep a lookout for wreckage or any papers etc. to identify a submarine blown up about 1.30 a.m. this morning."

Documents were recovered from several Zeppelins shot down on October 20 during a raid over France. *L49* was downed but not burned near Bourbonne-les-Bains (and near the American GHQ in France), and American searchers in a swamp found most pieces of the torn up North Sea chart (a directional chart for radio) as well as the basic codebook AFB and a new appendix of call signs.[132] Within a week after the chart was forwarded to Hall in London, he expressed his thanks "for this most valuable document, which I assure you will be of the greatest value."[133] In addition, there were two radio log books, a navigational log, and a weather code book.[134] British archives contain the *Navy List* with call signs, including those of U-boats, and a collection of Secret Orders.[135] British interrogators also obtained the log book of *L45*, soon sent to Marseilles by the French, but were aware that "one or two valuable notebooks" had been sent off to the French General Headquarters.[136]

Early in 1918 Valentiner of *U157* believed that the Gamma Ulli cipher had been broken, for in January a British submarine met *U156* at a rendezvous set up by radio.[137] On March 5 *U156* herself radioed cruiser command to obtain "key number for Gamma Ulli from March 4 on." The British intercepted and read her signal. On May 9 *U62* made a rendezvous with *U153*, and again a British submarine arrived on the scene. The wreck of *UB33* yielded basic books on May 21. She had sailed on April 6 and hit a Dover Barrage mine on April 11. The "materials" consisted of "a steel box containing signals books, codes, etc."[138]

A new signal book went into effect on June 1,[139] as the Admiralty had anticipated. Their worries on May 28 are reflected in a memorandum addressed to the Commander-in-Chief of the Grand Fleet and the Rear Admiral of the Harwich Force. The memorandum was written in Hall's style and read as follows:

> 1. The new German Signal Book comes into force at noon on June 1st. 2. Outpost boats should have this book on board on the night of May 31st-1st June and an endeavour will be made to obtain one by attacking the outpost boats off the Ems on that night. The attack will be carried out by the Harwich force. 3. Whether or not the attack on the outpost boats achieves its object it will greatly assist

the Special Branch of the Intelligence Division if the enemy are made to evince activity, with the increased signalling which it will entail, during the forenoon and afternoon of the 1st June.

The 20th Destroyer Flotilla Fast Division immediately proceeded to the Ems area to lay mines but without result. The destroyer *Shakespeare*, damaged by a mine, had to be towed home. On June 4 the Admiralty stated that the raid had been intended to obtain confidential books and to "occasion signalling in the middle of the day." The second goal was now said to have lost much of its value, but the first remained in effect, and the raid was to be repeated as soon as possible. Ten days later the operation was cancelled as "now less urgent,"[140] perhaps because documents from *UB33* had been read, or perhaps because of signals made by the Admiralty Staff on May 26 in both old and new keys and therefore readable.[141]

Beginning in late July, the Flanders command kept lists of secret documents aboard U-boats, all carrying AFB as well as selected *General Substitution Tables* for the cipher Gamma Alpha:

C, D, E, F aboard *UC49*, out August 1; D, E, F, G on *UB109*, out July 28; E, F, G on *UB57*, out August 3; *UB103*, August 14; and *UC70*, August 20; E, F on *UB30*, out August 6; only F aboard the small *UB12*, out August 19.

The boats also carried various editions of the substitution tables for Gamma Ulli. Editions 3 and 4, aboard *UB109* and *UC70*, were discovered in both wrecks, while the other boats carried only Edition 4, in effect since August 11 and due to expire at 0400 on October 21.[142]

During August and September the Germans introduced a new grid chart for the first time since the beginning of the war. It first appeared in British intercepts on August 13 when *UC71* made a Gamma Upsilon signal that could not be read in full and referred to a position as [1105] K. Instead of the areas indicated on the earlier charts, the new chart was divided into areas, denoted by letters, that contained 3000 numbered quadrants apiece.[143] By early September the new chart had replaced the old, fully known to the British after *UB109*, out July 27, was sunk off Folkestone on August 29 and divers recovered her secret documents between August 30 and September 4.[144]

On October 9 rather out-of-date documents appeared after the wreck of *UB110*, sunk on July 19, was towed to Newcastle on October 4. She was carrying AFB with substitution tables for Gamma Alpha, general substitution for AFB; Gamma Gamma, key procedures for AFB and FFB; Gamma Ulli for U-boats; and Gamma Omicron, keyword for superior officers.[145] *UC70*, out August 21 and sunk a week later, did not yield documents until October 14, when AFB with substitution tables was recovered. The tables were Gamma Alpha, versions E, F, and G; Gamma Ulli, editions 3 and 4 (good only until 0400 on October 21); Gamma Gamma; and Gamma Beta, key procedure for officers of higher rank.[146]

Not all these discoveries were equally valuable, and a great deal depended on chance -- along with the incessant work of decryption in London -- but the "miraculous" recovery of codes, cyphers, and call signs confirmed and facilitated the work of the cryptographers.

CALL-SIGNS

Reading call-signs meant being able to identify particular U-boats and trace their cruises. This task, highly important for taking countermeasures, was the responsibility of Fleet Paymaster E. W. C. Thring, in charge of Submarine Tracking. He probably compiled the informative Memorandum on Call-Signs in 1919. The first set of signs (captured, perhaps from *UB26*) was in use from the beginning of the war to April 1915; the second (worked out) until August 1. The third (worked out) was used until the beginning of 1916 and the fourth (captured from *L32*) until March 16 or 20. The fifth (worked out) was in force only from March 15 at noon until July 1 of that year. The sixth (worked out) lasted a little longer, until December 10, while the seventh (captured too late from *UC44*) was in effect until May 1, 1917.[147]

The new list then introduced contained four columns with four sets of names. Column 4 was valid from May 1 until July 1, but the British soon intercepted and identified three-letter signals beginning with FU (III Flotilla), LU (IV Flotilla), SX (II Flotilla), and VM (I Flotilla).[148] Later VF- was identified as a Flanders boat, LM- as one from Pola. Column 2 was valid for the period July 1--September 1. On July 1 the Admiralty warned that the first two letters of the 3-letter call signs were being changed from FV to OK (really FUbar to OK, III Flotilla) and LU perhaps to VA (IV Flotilla). The next day the statement was corrected to "VM apparently to FA" (really to NB), and more accurate correlations were worked out three days later: "VM to NB (I Flotilla), SX to FA (II Flotilla), FUbar to OK (III Flotilla), and LU probably to VA (IV Flotilla)."[149] This meant that the second column of the call signs was being substituted for the fourth.[150] Finally, Column 3 was good from September 1 only to November 10, when the DNI informed Admiral Beatty: "Enemy call signs changed at 11 a.m. today." A completely new name list was to be in effect until superseded on April 12, 1918.[151] Within four days the Admiralty were aware that call-letters beginning with ZL pointed to mine-laying submarines, while others were TH and RV (II Flotilla), XH and VJ (III Flotilla), YF (IV Flotilla), and QX (V Flotilla). FA indicated submarine cruisers, while UF and WH meant Flanders submarines of the I and II Flotillas.[152] It has been supposed that after the loss of four Zeppelins over

39

France on October 20 the German command considered the older tables compromised. (In fact, the British had obtained the book from *UC44*.) Whatever the reason, Column 1 was never used, and there was now a new three-volume list, with Volume 1 in force until April 12, 1918, volume 2 until September 21.

There were problems while Volume 2 was in force. On June 18, Captain James informed Admiral Beatty that "owing to great changes in Flotilla formations it is not possible to identify all boats,"[153] and though divers visited the wreck of *UC11*, out June 24, they found only a printed book with engineering details.[154] On the 29th the DNI informed Malta that "tables have changed; will send them out first opportunity, also keys."[155] On July 5 James told Beatty that "it is now considered possible to allocate enemy submarines to their proper George [letter] numbers with fair certainty."[156] On July 25 the Daily Submarine Return (see below) again uses call letters only, because the call-signs have changed once more.

Volume 3 was introduced at noon on September 21. It abandoned the old references to flotillas and boats in favor of call signs apparently random, and provided five different 3-letter signs for each boat.[157] The Submarine Return for the next day notes that "owing to change of call signs it is impossible for the time being to allocate call signs to submarines." Probably new calls could be correlated with old calls: "E.g. it appears that new FRW may be old Ubar QF." "Any suggestions for allocating new calls to old calls should be telegraphed to Admiralty," and on the 26th a telegram to Malta stated the Admiralty's "regret that call signs appear to be on entirely new principle with no flotilla indicator letters -- very difficult to distinguish at present."[158]

DECIPHERERS

A word should be added about the language experts who unravelled the cipher changes. Many of them were civilians, and were said to be the envy of other services. In the autumn of 1917 Admiral Sims wrote Captain Roger Welles, Director of Naval Intelligence in Washington, that

> at the British Admiralty they have a corps of grey-haired Oxford Professors, Egyptologists, Cuneiform Inscription Readers, etc., who break ciphers with great facility, and, I may add, have broken practically every cipher that they have been put up against.[159]

In reply, Welles claimed that he himself would soon rival the British Intelligence chief,[160] but his promise was not fulfilled because his materials were too sparse. British decryption was not based on purely mathematical or linguistic analysis, however. The constant search for wrecks shows that a great deal was learned from recovered books of codes and ciphers like those now preserved in the Public Record Office.

Sims noted the work of civilians, but they were not responsible for all decryption. Admiral James notes the vital work of Fleet Paymaster C. J. E. Rotter, "the principal German expert in the Intelligence Division."[161] Paymaster E. W. C. Thring analysed the call signals of the various U-boats, and Beesly tells how "in 1939, when he was sixty-four, [he] returned to re-form the Admiralty's Submarine Tracking Room."[162] The consequent "evasive routing" was already successful in 1917 and 1918 when he was at the Admiralty.[163] Indeed, during the Naval Investigation of 1920 Admiral Sims stated that "more shipping was saved through ...keeping track of submarines and routing ships clear of them than by any other single measure."[164]

THE DAILY RETURN

Toward the end of 1917 the Intelligence Division of the Admiralty compiled the *Daily Submarine Return*, including   all the times, locations, and much of the contents of U-boat signals, as well as notes on the number of days the boats had been on cruise. The *Return* contained most of the information communicated to Admiral Sims in the daily briefings at the Admiralty, where he or a deputy learned about British operations against U-boats and obtained some analyses based on decryption. (At the end of September 1918 Sims was simply told that the U-boats were not talking much.) One can check the dates of the decryption of some U-boat signals from the *Return* itself and from Sims's memoranda. Signals were not always read at once, sometimes not until long after interception.[165] Interrogation and decryption provided a great deal of information, but could not obtain detailed orders, log books, charts, or codes and ciphers.

Dorwart claims that the British were eager to "throw open secrets on cryptography,"[166] not necessarily all of them. Marder relates that "special intelligence on the U-boats was passed on to the French Naval Staff,"[167] but monthly charts of the Ministère de la Marine containing U-boat tracks show that while information about interrogations of prisoners was shared much else was not made known. Kahn says Hall told the French cryptographer Cartier that it was better to lose a French auxiliary cruiser than let the Germans know intelligence secrets.[168] A telegram of November 12, 1917, however, from Hall to Paris stated that a German submarine was "proceeding to Gulf of Lions and Genoa to attack expected transport of troops from Marseilles to Genoa." He added that "no submarine is there yet" and discussed the route the transport was expected to follow. This message must have been based on an intercept.[169] Hall had told the French that they would be informed about anything of importance to them, and he certainly valued their cooperation.

Meanwhile, of course, the French were reading on their own. Boucard quotes two signals from von Arnauld of *U35* and Steinbauer of *U47* (Austrian number for *UB47*) reporting that they had sunk French warships late in 1916. Both signals were read correctly.[170]

5. 1914-1916

We turn now to examine the activities of divers looking into U-boats and search parties investigating wrecked Zeppelins, hoping to see what results they achieved for naval intelligence.

MODERN DIVERS TO *U11*

U11 was mined off Zeebrugge as early as December 1914 but not investigated for more than eighty years. Then Belgian divers visited the wreck, in 5120/0252E, on the Ostend Bank, and recovered many small pieces. Stamped bits of metal clearly gave the submarine's number.[171]

FANTASY ABOUT *U31*

A widely circulated story about the first find of a U-boat wreck is legend, not history. The large new *U31* did vanish early in 1915 when she failed to return after sailing for the waters east of the Thames Estuary on January 13. In German circles the story somehow got started that she drifted ashore on the British coast with a dead crew, victims of suffocation, and Captain Gayer mentions it in a book published in 1920. German naval authorities soon asked the Admiralty about the narrative. Had *U31* "drifted ashore near Yarmouth intact with no water in the boat but with crew all dead on 14th or 15th March [1915]"? The Admiralty replied that there was no truth whatever to the story, and Fleet Paymaster Thring suggested that she might possibly have hit a German mine laid off Yarmouth in 1914.[172] The story itself seemed dead but was revived for a time in a 1937 book by "Clemens Laar" entitled *U31 Das Schiff aus dem Jenseits*. Bonatz says that the story was known in Berlin in August 1915, and then compounds confusion by discussing the materials aboard *U31* that must have fallen into British hands: secret documents including ciphering materials and charts of minefields. "It is not clear whether in consequence German keys were changed."[173] The whole sequence of events is fictional. A faint echo of it may perhaps be heard from prisoners from *UB26* who said under interrogation that "a German submarine has been lost off the British coast through the crew being drunk at night."[174]

NO CODES OR CIPHERS FROM *U8*

After *U8* (Stoss) was sunk off Dover by an explosive sweep on March 4, 1915, prisoners described how she had been sunk but reported that the war diary and signal books had been destroyed along with other papers. In any event the signal books would become "illegible on immersion." Later on, Dover authorities informed London that "books were thrown overboard before our boats could arrive."

The Admiralty had several schemes for dealing with the lost books. The day after the sinking they informed the Rear Admiral Dover that

> if the spot where officer of *U8* threw books overboard can be approximately located it will be worth while buoying the place and sending trawler to trawl there. A reward of thirty pounds may be promised to the boat recovering books.

The offer was cancelled the next day, however, as Captain F. W. Young of Admiralty Salvage was on his way to Dover. The salvage records do not show that he found anything of value. The wreck of *U8* has recently been rediscovered and identified again.[175]

A MYSTERIOUS WRECK FOUND LATER
U37 left Heligoland that March 20 for the Channel and sank several ships, the last two off Beachy Head on March 31 and April 1. Spindler notes that there is no record of a later encounter that might explain her loss.[176] Presumably it was due to accident. On September 3, 1917, however, a depth charge attack between Beachy Head and the Royal Sovereign Light Vessel seemed to result in a sinking, and divers sent down ten days later found an old submarine wreck at sixteen fathoms in Rye Bay between Hastings and Dungeness. The bows were buried in mud and the wreck was lying on her starboard side.[177]

Comparison with German records suggests that this may have been *U37*. Though by that time the minelayer *UC36* had also vanished in the Channel, apparently her location was nearer the Isle of Wight, and the distinctive bow of a minelayer might well have been recognized in spite of the mud.

Termote suggests that a wreck found on the Sandettie Bank is that of *U37*, but as he offers a choice between *U37* and *U31* we should opt for the latter.[178]

ACCIDENTAL RAMMING AND DISCOVERY OF A MINELAYER
At the end of May 1915 an Admiralty telegram noted the likelihood that German submarines would lay mines off the British coast. They carried no "minelaying apparatus" but might simply release drifting mines. In fact the first cruise of a minelayer from Flanders was made by *UC11* only a week later. One of her mines damaged a British destroyer at the southern entrance

to the Downs on June 1.[179] Further sinkings of East Coast shipping in June seemed due to mines laid in groups, and naval authorities guessed that steamers ostensibly neutral might be to blame.

Early in July, however, the true explanation came to light. Just before 3 p.m. on July 2 the small steamer *Cottingham*, bound from Calais to Leith, was in the Stanford Channel approaching Yarmouth Roads at 8 1/2 knots when she collided with a submerged object on the starboard quarter. There was no damage, but there was a smell of gas, and oil appeared on the surface. Later, when she was surveyed at Leith, it was found that her bottom had a "very slight graze and scratches." Soon after the collision two minesweepers swept over the position and their wires stuck fast at an obstruction. Indicator nets were laid at the spot and watch was kept. Six hours later there was a heavy underwater explosion and divers were sent down from HMS *Halcyon* and HMS *Dryad*, under Cdr. G. N. Ballard of *Halcyon*. They reported the wreck of a new minelaying U-boat on the bottom in only 9 1/2 fathoms, but very thick water and strong tides, with only about thirty minutes of slack each tide, made diving difficult. The divers stated that there were seven mine chutes; the foremost three contained mines while the four after chutes were empty. (Submarines of this class had six chutes, however, not seven, with two mines in each chute. If four chutes were really empty, she had laid eight mines.) Later accounts modified the description.[180]

A report from Lowestoft on July 11 stated that the U-boat had been blown up by one of its own mines. Forty-seven feet of the bow and central section, with conning tower, had been detached from the after part, not as yet located. There was no torpedo tube in the rounded bow, which had two plates, one on each side, two feet long by fourteen inches broad. A large hole extended from the stem on the starboard side, where the plates were much distorted and often showed jagged edges. Further investigation of this fore part revealed a cut about three feet into the superstructure before the conning tower, evidently caused when *Cottingham* ran over the submarine.

In the latter part of July they found the stern of the vessel with a hole about the whole diameter of the submarine. A diver got a little way into this and brought out some distorted pieces of accumulator. Portions of the wireless aerial were recovered, as well as bits of the sinker of another mine (presumably exploded) with part of the moorings attached. Several stanchions and stays and pieces of wire, presumably handrails, were also recovered.

One mine, live when found with its sinker complete, was recovered and forwarded to *Vernon*. The sinker was "a most complicated and ingenious mechanism... fitted with rollers to enable it to be either dropped or pushed out of a tube." Another live mine with sinker was somewhere in the vicinity. Patrols blew up two, while divers recovered two more with sinkers complete and found another sinker close to the wreck. The diver also reported that "the sea round about seems to be strewed with bits of twisted iron." By August 8 a diver got as far as twelve feet into the severed stern, finding mess tins and bits of clothing. He picked up fragments of accumulators from the batteries.

The Captain in Charge at Lowestoft suggested that the fore part of the submarine might easily be raised by wires passed through the mine chutes. "Perhaps a great deal of further interesting information could be obtained, and possibly the instructions for laying the mines and the positions in which they were to be laid would be found inside the vessel." A "private letter to the DID" is less optimistic. Part of the outer hull of the U-boat had been pulled up, with part of the upper deck and "covers for apertures." Presumably he is referring to the lifting of a "portion of outer skin (25 feet long x 9 feet broad), very much distorted, with several brass tallies." The whole hull was so distorted, however, that "it is difficult to tell exactly what would be underneath these." The distance from the bow to the chutes was twenty feet, thence thirty-three feet for seven [really six] chutes with iron gratings over the top. They had a diameter of 3 1/2 feet. Each of the first three still contained one mine, while the four after chutes were empty and the diver "could see right through." "In No. 1 mine hole a mine could be seen fairly close to top. Diver thinks about 10 inches down. In Nos. 2 and 3 mines apparently 2 feet down from top. He felt the bottom of the sinkers about 2 feet in from bottom." The empty chutes and shattered stern indicated that a mine had detonated under her. The distance from the last chute, past the conning tower to the break was 44 feet. There was "significant damage twelve feet abaft conning tower," where the wreck was " nearly cut in two." From break to stern was 66 feet. In the after part, within 12 feet toward the stern, a diver found bits of accumulators, some mess tins, and two fragments of clothing.

There is no record that any documents turned up, and the boat was identified as *UC2* (Mey) only later. She had arrived at Zeebrugge on June 26 and sailed three days later on her first cruise to lay mines in the Stanford Channel off Lowestoft. There she was accidentally run over but not severely damaged by *Cottingham*, only to fall victim to what Admiral Spindler calls a technical defect related to one of her mines.[181] Like *UC12*, she began laying from the chutes just before the conning tower.

In the *Official History* Corbett says the submarine was raised "shortly afterwards" and "from it was obtained our knowledge of the structure of the minelaying class."[182] His first statement is not correct. *UC2* was not raised but blown up, on the insistence of the Admiralty. What divers had reported about her, however, did lead to alterations in six of the E-Class submarines under construction. Their beam torpedo tubes were replaced by chutes in their saddle tanks and they carried twenty mines.[183] On July 12 Hall commented on the absence of a torpedo tube in the German vessel, evidently used only for minelaying. He added that the Intelligence Department had not heard of small submarines built in Belgium "operating in open waters." The next day Admiral Oliver approved ending the diving and blowing up the rest of the wreck, and the day after that the Commander-in-Chief of the Home Fleet informed all Naval Centres that "a report has been received of submarine minelayers being under construction in Germany. It is considered possible that some vessels of type mentioned have already been completed." As usual, "any facts tending to confirm this should immediately be reported to Admiralty for information of D.I.D."

On July 17 an Admiralty telegram ordered A. A. Ellison, Captain-in-Charge at Lowestoft, not to use an explosive sweep but to blow the wreck up with guncotton. The next day Hall recommended the award of 500 pounds to *Cottingham*. Evidently he had not yet learned that the submarine was sunk by explosion, not ramming, and later he reduced the amount to 200 pounds. With his usual desire for reticence, he added that "it would be well when giving the award to demand secrecy as to the locality."

Further minelaying activity was noted in a telegram to "all Naval centres" on July 19. "French Admiralty report that 7 German mines which from their mooring arrangements might have been laid by submarines, have been picked up off Calais during the last few days. D. I. D." In fact between the 12th and the 19th the French found eleven mines, while one more blew up a Belgian fishing boat. They concluded that they had been laid by an enemy submarine.[184]

Ellison was still trying to save the wreck as late as August 8. "It would not be difficult to raise the forepart [his letter still refers to seven vertical tubes, the three foremost with one or two mines each, while the four after are empty] as the wires could be passed through the tubes mentioned, and perhaps a great deal of further interesting information could be obtained, and possibly the instructions for laying the mines and the positions in which they were to be laid would be found inside the vessel." Hall replied at once. "Altho' there may be advantages in raising this wreck, there are also grave disadvantages -- and I think the latter are more important." Two days later, Admiral Oliver noted that "Captain-in-charge was ordered to blow up this wreck by Admiralty Telegram 385 of 17.7.15 and has delayed nearly a month in carrying out these orders. Submitted he be asked for an explanation. The Admiralty has good and urgent reasons for giving the order." Ellison gave in and on August 24 reported that 49 pounds of guncotton had been exploded in two tubes and the conning tower. Since two mines also blew up, the submarine was "now a shattered wreck." He persisted in pointing out that divers from Chatham earlier had attached wires to three German mines and got information about their construction, the number of mines, and the method of carrying them. On September 6 the Admiralty sent a secret letter of appreciation to the divers.

THE SELF-DESTRUCTION OF *UC12*

No further U-boat wrecks were investigated until another small minelayer, *UC12*, blew up on her own mines off Taranto on March 16, 1916, and was raised by the Italian Navy. This boat belonged to the same class as *UC2* and her contents were equally valuable, in spite of extensive damage. She had earlier laid mines in the Taranto area when she was in Austrian service as *UXXIV* (though with a German crew),[185] and then was rebuilt as a transport like her sisters *UC13* and *UC14* to carry weapons and ammunition to the Turks at Bardia on the Libyan coast. When restored as a minelayer she undertook minelaying cruises to Durazzo and Brindisi before returning to Taranto under Fröhner.[186] There she was laying mines under water when one of them exploded and threw up an immense column of water yellow with oil. Torpedo boats and harbour craft hastened to the spot, where air bubbles were bringing up pieces of wood and fragments of corpses. Divers went down at once and found the wreck in thirty-one meters. Sweepers found eight mines; two more had exploded and two were still in the foremost mine chute. Her twelve mines were thus accounted for. The wreck was raised in seventeen days, rebuilt, and commissioned in the Italian Navy as *X1*. Within it was found a copy of the Austrian *Offsekt code*, used at once by the Italians and sent on to London three months later. "It is believed that both signal book and cipher book are still in use. At any rate the Italians translate most of the current messages with little difficulty."[187]

Italian and British experts carefully studied the minelaying apparatus. When a mine was dropped, it went to the bottom with a sinker, to which the mine was rigidly secured. After a certain interval the pincer-like "grip" was released and the mine rose because of its positive buoyancy, remaining attached by a cable to the sinker on the bottom.

The mine could be released only when the two long arms of the "grip" were forced apart. Glycerine had to squeeze past a piston in a dashpot for about fifteen minutes before the arms could move. Again, the mine would not fire until it was freed from the sinker. A pin outside the detonator pocket prevented this from happening by accident. Finally, there was interlocking gear to prevent an upper mine from being dropped before the lower one.

How then could *UC12* have blown herself up? A British engineer reasoned thus.

> When the mine was dropped, the 'grip' immediately released owing to the dashpot not working correctly (e. g. glycerine may all have leaked away). The mine then rose and struck the submarine. N. B. Assuming that the mine which exploded was in the 2nd compartment from forward, and that the submarine was going 4

knots, about 8 seconds would elapse between the instants of releasing the mine and the explosion. [188]

The problem was to be important because *UC2*, *UC12*, and no fewer than five other UC-boats seem to have been sunk by their own mines. A warrant officer from *UC32* referred to the "interlocking gear...to prevent one of the upper mines being released before the mine or mines below it." After *UC65* was sunk toward the end of 1917 Lafrenz, her commander, stated that no changes had been made in the gear. An experiment with clockwork had been abandoned, and the Flanders minelayers continued to rely on dashpots with pure glycerine for a release thirty minutes after laying.[189]

SOME MATERIALS FROM A ZEPPELIN

On April 1 the Zeppelin *L15* was downed off the coast of Kent, and when the wreckage was towed on to Margate Sand investigators found one metal case with charts used by Zeppelins and U-boats, but no codebooks because the most secret documents had evidently been dropped into the Thames.[190]

CAPTURE AND INVESTIGATION OF *UB26*

A few weeks later the French were able to raise a submarine they had caught in a net. The "improved coastal submarine" *UB26* reached Zeebrugge from Kiel on March 21 and sailed ten days later under Metz to attack shipping off Le Havre. On April 4 the French received "secret information" about U-boats out from Flanders to operate off French ports, and early the next morning *UB26* was submerged near Le Havre when her torpedo missed a ship and thus alerted six British patrol drifters. The drifters shot their nets nearby, and while the U-boat was coming up from twenty meters to eleven she fouled the nets and struck the rudder of the drifter *Endurance*. She then went down to escape at twenty-seven meters but fouled another net and went to the bottom to wait for darkness before blowing tanks. After the French destroyer *Trombe* dropped three bombs on her estimated position, her battery caught fire and both propellers were finally entangled in the net. She came to the surface and surrendered before scuttling.

The French immediately raised the U-boat practically intact from a depth of only nineteen meters and found valuable documents inside it, sending the most important materials to the Admiralty on April 15.[191] These included charts of German minefields and buoys off the Belgian coast, estimated locations for the British net barrage there, and orders for U-boats operating in the Channel. The minefields included a large quadrilateral northwest of Zeebrugge as well as two lines north of Ostend and Zeebrugge, and three locations north of the Frisian Islands where U-boats acted as lookouts. Later the French authorities provided copies of these and other documents, as well as the radio equipment and even the flag of the submarine.

The Germans were expecting that the British would attack the Belgian coast as their fleet proceeded to the southern North Sea, and five UB-boats therefore left Zeebrugge on the evening of April 23 to take up stations between Harwich and Lowestoft. Early the next morning British forces began laying 1445 mines, mostly with nets, to the north and northwest of Zeebrugge. They could rely on the charts of German minefields just recovered.

Presumably *UB13* fell prey to the new British field, since she did not return to Zeebrugge. Later on the 24th five small minelayers tried to join the UB-boats but because of the nets three had to return to recharge their batteries. The next day, however, the larger *UB18* was able to torpedo *E22* off Braune Bank, taking two prisoners.

STRANDING AND CAPTURE OF *UC5*

UC5 under Mohrbutter was one of the small minelayers that went out from Zeebrugge but she fell into Allied hands a few days later. On the evening of the 26th she sighted an unfamiliar light vessel off the Galloper Shoal.

> 6.47 p. m. Galloper Sand buoys in sight. Proceeded along the Sand to ascertain the position of a newly placed light vessel. According to mean of positions the light vessel is at the north end of the shoal.

UC5 was unaware that in March the British had quietly moved several light vessels. At midnight she stranded on the sands, freeing herself six hours later with the rising tide. Later in the morning she was heading submerged toward another unmarked light vessel when she ran aground again. Though she surfaced she could not get off. Mohrbutter had the weighted signal book thrown overboard along with the machine gun and the small arms, and the minefield charts were burned. He then made a signal to inform Bruges that the submarine had been blown up near the southeast Shipwash buoy. The crew were safe but would be taken prisoner by the British.

Two British destroyers arrived on the scene after this message was intercepted, and then captured both submarine (not yet blown up) and crew. A prisoner advised his interrogator "to be careful when trying to raise *UC5*, as some of the mines had been released."[192] The diving party therefore lashed collision mats and wire nets under the hull to prevent the mines from dropping. Just before salvage tugs towed her off the sands into Harwich, the divers found the lost machine gun on the bottom, and local naval authorities were allowed to keep it for Shotley Museum. There is no indication, however, that the signal book turned up.[193] On May 22 -- nearly a month after the capture -- an Admiralty telegram informed the Commodore at Shotley that "all books and papers recovered from *UC5* should be sent without delay by hand to the Director of the Intelligence Division and every effort made to keep secret the fact that any documents have been recovered."[194] It is unclear exactly what did turn up. Certainly there was a diary of some sort, but presumably the most important documents had been destroyed.

Unlike *UC2* and *UC12*, this small minelayer was virtually intact, and her construction could be studied intensively. Such study was important because some features of the smallest minelayers would be preserved in the design of newer and larger sisters. The hull, later used to stimulate war-bond sales and recruiting, was sold for scrap at Montreal in 1923.

Two more Zeppelins were shot down during a raid on the East Coast in September. The wreckage of *L33* yielded the key to weather broadcasts, as well as radio log books, with her last signal at 10:58 "from DK to OK signed KK."[195] When the Zeppelin's surviving commander was interrogated he was shown not only plans of the latest Zeppelins but also a list of their radio call signs[196] -- presumably based on observation of signals. The other Zeppelin downed was *L32*, over South Green, near Billericay, where the codebook and war diary were recovered. Robinson comments thus:

> Nobody will ever know what caused Peterson, a very experienced commander, to take the new code along with him that night, particularly when the loss of the SL11 over London in flames three weeks before (of which he was an eyewitness) emphasized the danger of being shot down over land.[197]

Beesly says that this valuable book contained AFB, in use since March.[198] The war diary was also found, though "the edges, top and bottom of every page have been burnt away." The record ends at 12.35 a.m. on September 24, when the Zeppelin was over "Littlestone Point" and 800 kilometres from base.[199] She was set on fire about two hours later, after she had proceeded to Tunbridge Wells and then to the east and northeast of London.

Another Zeppelin, *L21*, was brought down in Hartlepool Bay on November 28 of the same year, but searchers were unable to find anything of value in the tangled mass of burned wreckage.[200]

No further U-boat or Zeppelin wrecks were investigated during 1916.

6. 1917

The setting for later diving operations was provided on January 25, 1917, when *Laurentic* was mined off Lough Swilly and, a week later, the First Sea Lord proposed to salve the guns "and other articles of value" from a depth of 120 feet. He stated that "Lieutenant Commander Damant, now serving in HMS *Excellent* and formerly Inspector of Diving, will be ... put in local charge of operations" in order to recover five million pounds' worth of gold bars aboard the steamer. Operations began February 21, but since Damant had to spend part of March working on the wreck of *UC32*, only four boxes had been brought up by April 24, leaving about two thousand more -- according to Admiral Oliver, who complained that "the Bank [of England] are always asking me about it," but said that Lt. D. W. McGuffie was working on it. Early in July Diver Miller, Carpenter RN, was appointed to *Laurentic* duty. On August 19 Damant proposed to use gelignite to open up the wreck, and at the end of the month 0.125 % of the gold was offered to the salvage party.

Damant went on leave September 18, just after 900,000 pounds sterling had been recovered. The weather was worsening, and decisions about further operations would be made only the next March.[201] Soon after he arrived at the mining school at Portsmouth he learned he was to report to the Admiralty and asked for Diver Miller for his new task on U-boat wrecks.[202]

INTELLIGENCE AND *UC39*

Divers were not immediately related to the case of *UC39* (Ehrentraut), which under attack from British destroyers off Flamborough surrendered to *Thrasher* on February 8. One destroyer removed seventeen Germans and two British prisoners while another took *UC39* in tow but was unable to bring her in to port. Her "log and charts and other documents" had already been captured and were sent to the Chief of the War Staff at the Admiralty two days later.[203] There was also a list of recognition signals, intended only for temporary use.[204]

Naval intelligence became further involved with this U-boat when one of her officers wrote home about the qualms he felt about shelling the neutral steamer *Ida*. Hall was asked if the intercepted letter could be used for propaganda and refused permission, though he was willing to transmit it officially to the Norwegian government. In addition, in the mail he received an anonymous letter addressed to "Secretary, Intelligence Department, Admiralty, London W," stating that "the enclosed was picked up in the street on Saturday morning and forwarding it in case it should be of some use." What was enclosed was a crumpled copy of orders for the Submarine School at Kiel on January 15. "Without doubt," Hall commented, "it was dropped -- crumpled up into a ball -- by a member of the crew of *UC39*, when they were being conveyed across London." [205] Sixteen months later divers visited the wreck, but it was too old to be worth investigating.

DIVERS AND THE LOSS OF *UC32*

Another sinking off the coast was due to a U-boat's own mines. On the evening of February 23 *UC32* was on the surface, running parallel to the Sunderland breakwater and only three hundred yards away. Her commander, Breyer, later reported that he had already laid six mines just off the mouth of the Tyne, though since fourteen mines remained in the chutes he had laid three and was either confused or trying to mislead his captors. He also stated that just after he laid his first mine off Sunderland there was a violent explosion under the hull. "The boat suddenly heeled over, stern seemed to break away from rest of boat." Breyer and one of the two men with him on the conning tower found themselves in the water. A stoker joined them after he heard the explosion, saw water pouring in and felt the boat sinking. Air pressure forced him into the conning tower and thence into the sea. An examination vessel from Sunderland picked these three up.

The next day a chain sweep located the wreck, but a report on the 26th indicated difficulties. "Divers can only feel the wreck, water from River Wear being very thick." The next day, however, a diver was able to find iron gratings apparently covering the mine chutes and bring up a "small piece of pressure hull, indicating extensive damage." The deck gun and its mounting were intact. On the 28th divers located the conning tower, two intact periscopes, and the conning tower hatch, which was open but too small for a diver in suit to enter. The hull had been severely damaged near the engine room. On March 1 about thirty feet of the stern turned up, with rudder and propeller, separate from the bow. The forward portion of the U-boat had not been damaged. Meanwhile, as the weather worsened, "small trawling nets were towed continuously round wreck for books, loose gear, etc., with no result up to date."

After a gale removed all buoys and marks, Damant arrived at Sunderland for further investigations and on March 18 decided to salve a torpedo after a diver reported finding the rear door of the starboard bow tube. Twelve hours later it was safe on the surface with its warhead and pistol intact. By the end of the month, however, it became clear that nothing new could be expected from the wreck. Damant reported that "there are still 14 unexploded mines in the fore part, which would render any lifting operations most hazardous to the vessels and crews employed. It is therefore proposed to abandon salvage operations and explode the mines with a charge." After further reflection on the "nearly two tons of explosive" in the wreck, the Admiralty decided not to try to blow it up. By this time the divers had gained considerable experience in dealing with a U-boat wreck. Not only the torpedo but also the "Machinery History" of the vessel came into British hands.[206] The recovery of more important documents remained a goal for the future.

Obviously the minelayer's own mine had blown up (the one at the bottom of the fifth chute), and a signal intercepted from her sister *UC33* (Arnold) on February 20 reflected a similar experience. She had laid only fifteen mines, "as one [bottom of the bow chute] detonated immediately on being thrown; returning via Shetlands owing broad oil track."[207]

DOCUMENTS FROM THE WRECK OF *UC61*

Another Intelligence achievement did not involve divers. Early on the morning of July 26 the outward-bound *UC61* radioed to Bruges that she was aground near Boulogne and could not get off. (Bartenbach noted that French radio placed her near Gris Nez, not Boulogne.) Her crew blew her up with bombs that "entirely destroyed the central part of vessel and started a fire which burnt out the whole interior of the hull."[208] French investigators found the commander's notebook indicating the harbours where German mines had been reported. The British had found them in a circular area east of Beachy Head (July 23), northwest of Cherbourg (July 21), south of Brighton (July 16), and northwest of Fécamp (July 10). Obviously the Germans had been reading encoded Admiralty warnings. There was also a sketch that showed the mines laid by *UC62* near the Royal Sovereign Light Vessel on June 23.

On August 4 the notebook was given to British authorities at Dunkirk and immediately sent across to Dover. Three days later, Vice-Admiral Bacon telegraphed the Admiralty about the consequences.

> From papers found in *UC61* it is evident that she had information of the danger areas declared on the 23 July when she left on the 24 July. This shows that the auxiliary code or vocabulary signal book is useless as a code. I have given orders that the fact of any area being declared *clear* is not to be passed by W/T.[209]

Hall evidently relied on Bacon's discovery when he telegraphed Paris that evening.

> Vice-Admiral Dover reports that documents from *UC61* show that Germans have information about our minefields etc which they probably got from one of our codes being compromised. Please procure me either original or true copies -- not translations-- of documents -- matter is urgent.[210]

Hall's memorandum of August 9 was also based on Bacon's work. "It would appear that the Germans have decoded our signals.... The codes concerned can be ascertained from Vice Admiral Dover." Five days after that, the Signal Section reported having taken "necessary steps."[211]

They had moved faster than that, for by August 10 the German Admiralty Staff concluded that the British knew that their cipher for the Auxiliary C-14 Code was compromised, since they had undertaken a wholesale change of ciphers. The Staff asked Bruges if *UC61* was carrying decryption materials which might have fallen into British hands. The reply was that the commander, K/L Gerth, was a former radio officer and officer on the Admiralty Staff and must surely have destroyed secret documents of this sort.[212] No reference was made to his notebook.

THE SINKING OF *UC44*

On the night of August 4-5 Tebenjohanns in *UC44* laid four mines to the west of Waterford harbour entrance and then proceeded under water to the centre in order to lay five more. As the ninth mine cleared -- the top mine in the fourth chute from the bow -- there was a violent explosion under the stern and the boat dropped to the bottom in twenty-five meters. Tebenjohanns and two others got out through the conning tower hatch, but he was the only one still swimming an hour and a half later when a lifeboat came out. Its crew were astonished to find that they had rescued a U-boat commander.

What had caused the demise of *UC44*? The question is closely related to what the Germans may have known about British minesweeping. Tebenjohanns thought one of her own mines had detonated under her. Arnold, the commander of *UC33*, believed that *UC44* had been sunk because the British could anticipate overly methodical minelayings. Arnold's view has held the field ever since. Hurd gives it in its simplest form: "It appeared that her captain was unaware that mines had recently been laid in that locality." Gibson and Prendergast speak of a dummy counter-mining sweep. James adds that the German signals showed that the code for reporting mine clearance was compromised. A clearance signal was therefore made, he says, and Waterford was closed for two weeks until *UC44* arrived and hit the unswept mines. Beesly follows James but adds that the British learned of the broken code when listening to "Norddeich's broadcasts of Neumünster information."[213] One more version appears in Hall's own reminiscences.

A submarine minelayer with the greatest regularity used to lay 18 pills every six weeks outside Waterford Harbour. Admiral Preston was informed that she would arrive on a certain Monday night. She was blown up. The Commanding Officer and one other officer were the only ones saved. Former came to tea with me next day and said, only possible solution was, 'Your mine-sweepers don't sweep!' But it was only a dummy mine-sweeper! The German officer said he would send the information home if he could, and he was allowed to do so.[214]

It is true that on August 10 an interrogator was asking Tebenjohanns about clearance signals, inquiring "whether he was able to read British wireless messages giving the danger zones." The German commander "replied that as an officer he could not answer this question; from the expression on his face, however, it appeared that this was the case and that they are able to read our warnings."[215] The question shows that by the 10th the Admiralty were concerned with the clearance signals. Since Bacon first suggested on August 7, however, that the Germans were reading these signals, Waterford Harbour is not likely to have been closed earlier, and the interrogator must have been checking on the general decryption situation, not the sinking of UC44. The sequence of events means that British mines cannot have been left in an area supposedly swept in order to sink this submarine on August 4.

Sometimes, of course, mines were left unswept because not found. UC42 had laid mines in the entrance to Waterford Harbour on June 14, six of them less than a mile from the location where the wreck of UC44 would lie.[216] These mines were not found at once, for on July 12 the trawler George Milbourn was sunk on one of the six off Dunmore. At that point, however, the harbour presumably was swept.

The damage discovered later indicates clearly that one of UC44's own mines exploded.

> Her stern is blown up. Bulkhead at after end engine room crumpled and practically the whole of stern abaft the bulkhead wrecked. Damage to bottom extends well forward under engine room.

In addition, the British swept up precisely eight mines in the locality, and the fact that the ninth mine could not be found shows that it was responsible for the sinking.

One mine did not drop on another. Cdr. Heaton's report (October 12) on the removal of the mines from the submarine showed how difficult this would have been. "On starboard side of each tube a simple locking arrangement is fitted, to assure that no mine can be released until the mines below it have been laid and their side grab stops withdrawn."[217]

THE SALVAGE OF *UC44*

The Admiralty insisted on a vigorous search as soon as the U-boat was sunk. The next afternoon the First Sea Lord told Queenstown that

> it is very important to locate wreck of German submarine off Dunmore if possible so that if in suitable depth diving operations may be undertaken. Also most important that no information should get out as to how or where she was destroyed.

On the 6th Queenstown reported that "wreck of German submarine located and buoyed in 14 fathoms, sandy bottom, damage apparently slight. Racer from Berehaven, lifting craft is being sent from Holyhead." In his reply the First Sea Lord still laid emphasis on the papers.

> Our principal object is recovery of all books and documents. We hope to get valuable information. Please send any recovered direct to me by hand. Utmost secrecy is of course essential. Will reply about salvage later. Meanwhile could diver examine with a view of getting at books etc if possible.[218]

As the Admiralty began considering salvage, two divers who had worked on *UC5* were summoned to Waterford and the long task was begun. Because of bad weather, the wreck was not lifted until September 7, or brought into Dunmore Harbour until the 23rd. "Top of hull just awash at low water today." By the 28th seventeen bodies had been recovered, two more the next day when "a large quantity of important matter" was also obtained. Five days later all the mines and torpedoes were out, and on October 5 there were further confidential documents to be sent to Whitehall. The Admiral at Queenstown listed items in a telegram to the DNI.

> Commander Roe of my staff is due at Euston 6am.tomorrow Saturday with following salved from German submarine *UC44*. One map showing approximate tracks of previous cruises of submarine. Two cases of charts. One case of miscellaneous letters &c. He also has three cases containing complete wireless installation of submarine.[219]

Among the many valuable documents found in *UC44* special attention was given to AFB with "alterations" (enciphered) from May 31, 1917, to January 20, 1918, now at Kew; the *Tactical Organization* for February 8 (listing U-boats by flotillas) and the call sign list of May 1, with amendments;[220] and orders of the BdU. On May 8 Admiral von Holtzendorff had discussed the treatment of American ships. Since the United States had not officially informed either Germany or Switzerland about a state of war, "we are not at war with the United States of America," and outside the "barred area" ships bound for America were to be treated "as if the United States were a neutral country."[221] There was also the record of a conference with the Commanding Officer, U-Boats, on January 17, 1917, with the order that all submarines were to pass through the English Channel, moving westward past the North Hinder Light Vessel, Buoy 2501, and the light buoys in the Straits of Dover "without being observed and without stopping." U-boats going round Scotland, on the other hand, were "to let themselves be seen as freely as possible in order to mislead the British."[222] The log book from November 4, 1916, to August 4, 1917, was also found, ending with 2040 on August 4: Newton Head bearing 336 degrees, Hook Point 48 degrees, and 2242: Lay on the bottom in 12.5 fathoms, just before going up to lay mines.

Among the miscellaneous papers were orders related to the "central boat" to be stationed west of Ireland to observe shipping. Submarines not receiving news from Bruges and the *Arkona* "should request the central boat to transmit such signals again," in AFB enciphered Gamma Ulli. Special call signs were to be used "to conceal the increased wireless traffic of the central boat."

The radio equipment of *UC44* was sent to the Signal School.[223] It "had apparently been immersed in sea-water mixed with oil for a considerable time. All the parts took many days to dry out and the large amount of wood and the form of papier-mache used in the construction had deteriorated badly." The tuning of the transmitter was especially interesting, since it could be set to send on wave lengths of 300, 360, 400, 530, 600, 670, 740, and 820 meters.

The acoustic gear was compared with British counterparts and judged inferior, in spite of the fact that it "was supposed to have a range of between 20 and 25 nautical miles and to be able to determine direction and character of the sound source."[224]

DIVERS AND THE WRECK OF *UC41*

Another minelayer, *UC41*, met her end off Scotland in August, presumably because one or more of her own mines exploded prematurely, but very little was found in the wreck. On the 21st three minesweepers were at work off Dundee when one noted an explosion nearby and saw oil coming up. When they swept the waters nearby they fouled an obstruction, and after they finished, a German mine came to the surface and they proceeded to drop depth charges. There was a violent explosion, possibly due to a mine within the U-boat since oil and air bubbled up. After a total of seven depth charges there was yet another underwater explosion, and the sweepers picked up some woodwork. Listening on hydrophones, they could hear electric motors running for two hours. Sweepers later found two more German mines and by August 30 divers had located the wreck. That day they examined it from the stem to a point ten feet abaft the conning tower. They found a break about eight feet long on the starboard side aft and another small fracture on the superstructure still farther astern. A week's work showed that the U-boat had been cut through about forty feet abaft the conning tower.

A few days later investigations showed that the first three chutes from the bow still held their mines, while there was one in the fifth chute, none in the sixth. (Presumably the mines found came from the sixth chute.) Oddly enough, nothing was reported about the fourth, where the trouble may have occurred. The whole salvage effort was handled badly, however, and the situation may not have been described correctly. An Admiralty telegram to Aberdeen on September 17 was unduly optimistic. "When German submarine is salved all papers books and documents are to be carefully collected and sent by hand of an officer direct to Director of Intelligence, Admiralty" with the "utmost secrecy."[225] No such documents became available.

Lt. McGuffie, salvage officer who had been made Acting Commander for work on this submarine, had disagreements with the divers but was eager to keep at it until something important was found. As late as September 29 he telegraphed to London, "Work carried out this afternoon was very satisfactory." The Admiralty replied in the negative. "Operations are to be abandoned as ordered. It is not considered desirable that they should be continued." McGuffie did not give in without a struggle. That day he telegraphed thus: "Lieutenant George has left with books etc. Omitted to tell him I have retained one book copy 1892 pending further instructions in this case." It is not clear what "copy 1892" was. Early in October McGuffie made four more reports on supposed discoveries, but finally the Admiralty had to inform him that "in view of instructions to abandon salvage operations your telegram not understood." The work was terminated.[226]

The records suggest that this venture had been a waste of time except for confirming the sinking of a submarine minelayer. Analysis of call signs later identified the boat as *UC41* under Förste.

THE SELF-DESTRUCTION OF *UC42*

Yet another minelayer was found near the entrance to Queenstown Harbour a month after *UC44* had been raised. On October 31 the obsolete small torpedo boat *TB055* was escorting minesweepers in the channel south by east of Roch Point, an area swept every day because of German mining against the important traffic there. Near the end of the sweep was practically over," *TB055* sighted an oil track[227] and stopped to listen on her hydrophone, with surprising results. She heard a high-pitched sound as of a turbine engine, along with frequent noises from knocking or hammering; twice the hydrophone picked up what sounded like a radio transmission. The torpedo boat then dropped a depth charge that brought oil and air to the surface. Soon afterwards the trawler *Sarba* dropped another depth charge, and much more oil and air came up. The next day sweepers found an obstruction, and the day after that, a diver was sent down. He reported finding the wreck of a submarine lying on her side, at a depth of thirteen fathoms. According to Chatterton he also brought up the boat's starboard sidelight, with the number '42', which at first suggested *U42*.[228] The Admiral at Queenstown informed the First Sea Lord that "Submarine outside Queenstown appears to be almost buoyant. Would you like her lifted and brought in to harbour if it is possible with our appliances? We could probably get valuable papers out of her also periscopes." The reply was negative. "I do not propose to bring her in. We have all [the] information we are likely to get and the knowledge that we had recovered her might lead to a change of codes, etc., which it is most desirable to avoid." Indeed, the German call signs were changed three days later.[229]

DIVERS TO *UC42*
A whole day's diving off Queenstown on November 13 allowed the naval authorities to send detailed information to the Admiralty.

> Number on brass plate on top of conning tower is C42, 1916. Wreck has six mine tubes. Foremost tube is empty, remainder are full. Two torpedo tubes forward, as in *UC44*, upper deck steering position being before the windscreen, on a high step. Highest part of conning tower has apparently three hatches leading to it, and is reached by iron ladders bolted on each side aft. Stern is blown off. Impossible to obtain her length. Two hatches, one on conning tower and one just before the gun are now open. Two periscopes down, fore periscope port side, mast starboard side of steering compass. An attached sketch shows the large hatch aft closed.

Two days later London was able to inform Admiral Sims that "an enemy submarine has been located on the bottom in the vicinity of Daunt Rock, but whether she was sunk by depth charges or through striking a mine is not known." In fact, one of her own mines had blown up under her. It is not clear why she began minelaying from the bow chute.

Hall had firm ideas on the subject.

> This submarine is now supposed to be *UC42* from the plate with C42 on the conning tower. The fact of hatches being open seems to show that she reached the surface after the explosion, but as the

event probably occurred at night, any men who may have got out had not much chance of being saved. *UC42* must have been dead long before *TB055* and *Sarba* saw the oil and dropped the depth charges. In view of the possibility of this being some other submarine than *UC42* ask C. in C. Queenstown if he can recover anything from her with the actual number of the submarine on it.

It is uncertain that divers acquired a "fresh haul of papers," as suggested by Patrick Beesly. What they discovered on December 11 was a buoy with telephone and signal light. It bore the inscription in German, "Submarine C.42 sunk here. Immediately telegraph location to submarine command Kiel." The submarine was thus finally identified; she was *UC42* under Müller. At some point a torpedo was also brought up and given to the Americans at Queenstown. It was "fitted with appliance that none of our experts could tell the use of, maybe for passing under hull and exploding." (Presumably the experts were able to identify it as a magnetic pistol, if it was one.) Both buoy and torpedo came from outside the hull of *UC42*, not inside it.

During December the Germans received some information about the sinking of *UC42*, though they could not possibly have recognized it as such. American prisoners taken from the destroyer *Jacob Jones* by *U53* revealed that at the end of October a minelaying U-boat was sunk by depth charges. There were no survivors, but the sinking was confirmed by divers. At Bruges the command suggested that the vessel in question was *UC63*, lost around that time, but the Americans had given the date of discovery as the date of loss. It is not clear how the British determined that the submarine was sunk on September 10, but they did so before the end of December. The summaries in ADM 137/3918 suggest that they first supposed that *UC42* was the submarine possibly on her way to Queenstown when attacked by *Viola* on the morning of September 9, and then noted that there were no traces of her activities after the 10th. (She had left Heligoland for Irish waters on September 1.)

WAS THERE A TRAP FOR *UC42*?

Hall thought that *UC42* blew up on one of her own mines. It is likely, as we have seen, that such was the fate of *UC44*. Several authors have suggested, however, that *UC42* hit German mines previously laid in the area but not swept up by the British, either intentionally or by accident. The exact location of the wreck, which limits the range of possibilities, was 514530 N./081315 W, according to Dewar's revised and accurate list. This differs from the location supplied to Spindler,[230] and it means that the only German field close by consisted of four mines laid by *UC33* on August 11 in 514440 N./0813 W., close to the wreck. It is most unlikely, however, that a mine in such a field, and so small a field at that, caused the sinking. The wreck lay "close at the edge of the swept channel" leading into Queenstown. This channel was swept daily, and no ship had been sunk in it since March 7. Obviously the sweeping was highly effective and continuous. It could hardly have been abandoned in the hope of trapping a U-boat some day.

As for the very idea of trapping, we recall that Hall's memorandum about German decryption of British minesweeping signals was written only on August 9. It would have been impossible to stop sweeping mines off Queenstown by August 10 or so. These points confirm the conclusion that UC42 blew up on her own mines.

A TRAP FOR UC6

We have seen that minelayers on the Irish and Scottish coasts were wrongly thought to have been trapped by British actions. On the East Coast, however, UC6 was certainly trapped. During 1917 the Admiralty carefully studied patterns of minelaying in coastal waters and were able to tell Admiral Sims that "minelaying submarine commanders are specialists for certain localities." In this situation, they could look for a submarine or submarines that laid mines in the Thames Estuary almost weekly from April onward. Would one not be likely to return in late September? British minelayers acted rather late in the day when they deposited 120 mines in nets to the south of the Kentish Knock Light Vessel on the morning of September 27, but that very afternoon UC6 (Reichenbach) -- responsible for most of the earlier activities -- arrived in the vicinity and was heard by the Light Vessel before she continued under water. About two hours later, and again an hour after that, the Light Vessel heard a total of eight underwater explosions that must have accounted for her.

On November 21 the Weekly Report noted that no mines had been found in the vicinity of the Nore since September 24, and "as it is well known that minelaying submarine commanders are specialists for certain localities, a possible explanation may be the loss of the boat or boats particularly detailed for this area." UC11 had taken over the minelaying task, but only on November 13.

Some of the nets hauled up nearby in January 1918 contained bits of exploded mines, a twisted German mine-sinker, three pieces of plate, and a part marked Schmierröhre Anker Winde or Capstan Lubricating Pipe. Obviously the submarine perished in this location, perhaps first striking British mines and then touching off some of her own.

The development in British methods deserves notice. At first the losses of little minelayers off the East Coast were due to accident, as in the case of UC2. One cause of the capture of UC5 had been accident, another the moving of light vessels to produce stranding. Now in the case of UC6 the

British carefully laid mines where she might be expected to return. The later sinking of *UC11* in these waters reflects similar ingenuity.

THE SINKING OF *U58* OFF QUEENSTOWN

Minelayers were not the only submarines sunk off the southern coast of Ireland in the autumn of 1917. On the afternoon of November 16 a signal was picked up from IOL (*U58*), evidently heading west from the Channel approaches toward Ireland. She arrived off Queenstown that day and was captured on the next by the American convoy-escort destroyer *Fanning* (Lt. Cdr. A. S. Carpender, USN) but then sank. The submarine's roster went down with the one man drowned, while survivors claimed they had passed north of Scotland and knew the convoy's sailing time.[231]

Hall immediately telegraphed Queenstown. "Can wreck of submarine be located? Matter is important in view of change of call signs" -- changed on November 10. The local Admiral's reply missed the point. "Divers have visited *UC42* as previously reported. Work on her has now been stopped since she is not to be lifted." The Admiral evidently recognized his error, however, and sent another message the same day. "There are twenty-nine fathoms of water in position where obstruction has been located." Now he was thinking about *U58*, but he suggested that it was impossible to visit or raise the wreck.

DIVERS TO *UC47*?

UC47 was sunk off Flamborough Head on November 18, and though there seems to be no record of any investigation of the wreck, Spindler was informed that British divers brought up charts on which were marked the minefields laid by *UC47* off Guernsey on July 16 and off Cherbourg on September 24.[232] On the other hand, British wartime records do not identify the wreck as *UC47*, and as late as December 15 Intelligence supposed that she was a UB-boat.[233] When were the charts found? Under what circumstances? Divers were not likely to dive to twenty-five fathoms out in the North Sea. Perhaps a depth charge or sweep was used to blow the wreck open.

THE MINING OF *UB81*

Off the Owers on December 2 the new *UB81* under R. Saltzwedel struck a mine with her stern at twenty-five meters; water began to enter and the door to the next compartment forward was closed. Sprung rivets let the water spread. Saltzwedel used the remaining air pressure to blow the forward diving tank, and thus brought the submarine to a 53-degree angle in 28 meters. Since the cap of one bow torpedo tube was three meters above the surface, the torpedo was taken below and three men attached a tackle outside. Seven more were lifted up and out, but three went down again because of the cold. After six hours, star signals and a searchlight finally attracted the attention of the British patrol boat *P32*, but as she came close, wind and sea forced her on to the U-boat's bow, which disappeared under water with the tube open. There were six survivors.

DAMANT AND THE SEARCH FOR *UB81*

Damant came to the fore with the search for the wreck of *UB81*. He had been sent to the mine school at Portsmouth during October and reported to the Admiralty on November 27 just in time to look for *UB81* from December through February.[234] Portsmouth reported initial success on December 10: "German submarine *UB81* has been definitely located by divers in 15 fathoms about 136 degrees 10 1/2 miles from Dunnose. Weather is interfering with further operations." The Admiralty optimistically inquired, "Can papers be salved without raising or can submarine be brought into shallow water?" and then made the request, "Please raise submarine if possible, doing all that is practicable to preserve secrecy." Finally, however, the wreck was lost in heavy weather and the search came to an end.[235] Today "this vessel has received the attentions of commercial salvage," and the wreck lacks bow, stern, and conning tower, though "she makes an excellent wreck for sports divers."[236]

THE DOVER BARRAGE BEGUN

British mines earlier laid near the Straits had been notoriously ineffective because they failed to detonate on contact, and two area sinkings toward the beginning of the war were not due to them. During 1916 and early 1917 minefields and nets laid east of the Straits were easily spotted and almost useless.

During 1917, however, the British began to make new and improved mines, set off by chemical horns copied from captured German models, and the Dover forces began laying them toward the French side of the Straits. Another difficulty then arose. Vice Admiral Bacon at Dover was unwilling to use lights with his patrols because of the danger of attack by German destroyers. His hesitation was reasonable in view of German raids during 1917 (and again in 1918), but the gain from forcing U-boats to dive into the mines at night was likely to outweigh losses.

Papers taken from the wreck of *UC44* helped solve the Admiralty's problem. They had mistakenly believed with Bacon that the larger U-boats were passing north of Scotland, but in fact U-boat orders told them to move unobtrusively through the Straits and show themselves when taking the northern route. As early as August 21, however, Captain W. Fisher, Director of the Anti-Submarine Division, had reported to the Chief of the Naval Staff that the stranding and capture of *UC61* showed it was a "delusion that submarines operating in the Channel proceed thither north about." He appended a table of transits from January to August which showed that a total of 27 boats were "certain" to have passed outward through the Straits, 39 more were "probable," and another 13 were "possible." [237] In September 1917 the German orders were found in the wreck of *UC44*, but Bacon paid no attention to the discovery and insisted that the old barrage east of Dover had been a success. In January when Roger Keyes succeeded him, he was amazed to find the German orders in Bacon's safe, along with "all the information supplied by the Naval Intelligence Department, regarding the ceaseless and unrestricted procession of submarines."[238]

At the end of November, however, the Channel Barrage Committee, headed by Keyes, presented a report Hall supplied with an appendix on U-boat movements through the Straits. This was based on a German analysis, found in *UC44*, that had been made at the end of May in order to encourage commanders of the larger U-boats to take the Straits route.[239] The report began with the German figures totalling 147 transits during February through May and compared them with results "based on visual reports and a few directionals" from January through May, totalling 131. The total was then divided into "by day 3, by night 128" (adding up to 131) and then "not stated 16" was added in order to reach the German total of 147. Perhaps by coincidence the figure 16 was the same as the British figure for the month of January, not included in the "captured documents." In addition, it was noted that 29 crossings took place on the surface, 9 submerged. These figures came from "Experiences of German Submarines, November 1916--June 1917," another document found in *UC44*. They could not be coordinated with the table, and therefore Intelligence added, in order to reach the German total of 147, that probably 109 crossings took place on the surface. The figures for June and the period August 1--November 14 were British and came exclusively from observations, with July unfortunately lacking. The total came to 106. The sum of the two totals thus became 253.[240]

This list was obviously flawed. It was not prepared for historians of the Straits but for students of conflict within the Admiralty. It really did show that U-boats passed through the Straits with ease. Bacon was wrong when he refused to use flares and searchlights before mid-December.

THE SINKING OF *UB56*

Under pressure from Keyes the Admiralty explicitly ordered Bacon to illuminate the minefield, and he first did so on the night of December 17-18. The very next night, Hans Valentiner, outward bound in *UB56*, must have sighted the lights near the NE Colbart Buoy and decided to dive. Soon afterward he hit a mine nearby and a violent explosion shook the destroyer *Gipsy*, which heard men shouting twenty minutes later and with her searchlight was able to sight two swimmers. She could pick up only one, who died within the hour. "His clothes, marked 'Bleeck,' prove him to have been a German Engine-Room Petty Officer," says the report. He was Max Bleeck of *UB56*. He was picked up "about one mile southwest of the nearest deep mine," but the tide was "setting strong to the southwest" and the detonation obviously took place well to the northeast.[241] The next morning Bacon telegraphed to the Admiralty: "I think it would have a good effect if a thousand pounds for sinking submarine was approved by wire and distributed among the six nearest drifters."[242] The wreck was found in August but not identified.[243]

When the sinking of *UB56* indicated that Bacon's judgment had been wrong, Keyes took his place at Dover. At the same time Bacon's supporter, the cautious and pessimistic Admiral Jellicoe, was also replaced.

7. 1918

TWO MISTAKEN CLAIMS

Because Keyes owed so much to the work of divers, especially those who dealt with *UC44*, he was convinced that sinkings could be proved when wrecks were visited and therefore insisted too much on such proof supposedly provided in the Straits in January 1918. According to him, divers visited and identified the wrecks of *UC50* and *U109*.[244] In fact, *UC50*, out from Zeebrugge under Seuffer, to the French west coast on January 7, was not visited. It is not likely that west of Gris Nez on January 8 *UC50* caused an explosion that brought oil and fish to the surface, for there were no mines in the reported locality. But since no evidence suggests that she reached the Biscay area, she may have struck a mine somewhere after all.

The other boat, *U109*, sailed from Borkum on January 24 on her maiden voyage and was not heard from afterwards. She had a difficult transit. Two Admiralty telegrams of January 23 speak of her escorts. The first of them describes the "Third TBD Half Flotilla" as proceeding "to Borkum for escorting, the special orders are undecipherable but apparently refer to escort out of *U109*." The second says that "nine destroyers of 1st Flotilla have orders to escort *U109* and *UB67* out on Mall on 24 January. They pass Riff Gat [western Ems estuary] at 1300." The "Mall" or Yellow route, freshly swept after the sinking of *UB22* on "Kingsway" or Middle, was temporarily in use again.

On the 27th, however, Hall apparently told Sims that *U109* was "proceeding through the northern North Sea closer to Scotland than usual" and recalled that she "would not go out with five destroyers, demanded nine." Was she heading round the north of Scotland? Ney, her commander, had been left free to choose his route[245] and could have headed north, avoiding the Straits entirely. But perhaps the reference to Scotland is due to a misunderstanding, since no such reference occurs in the original translations of signals from *U109*.

A U-boat was almost certainly sunk northwest of Gris Nez on January 26 after the drifter *Beryl III* sighted a very big submarine with two deck guns heading slowly westward in a morning fog and drove her under with gunfire. Two hours later there was a heavy underwater explosion about three miles to the northwest. Probably the same boat caused it.

On February 5 Keyes told Hall that four witnesses had studied photographs and silhouettes and agreed that the boat resembled *U33/36*. "All added that the conning tower and bridge was in one single vertical line instead of in two steps as shown in this photo [of the earlier class] and that her sheer forward was higher than shown in picture, both these characteristics I believe to exist in higher numbered enemy submarines, they all spoke of her great length."

In his memoirs Keyes confidently stated that later on "divers were sent down and she was identified as *U109*."[246] Though no divers' reports confirm his statement, *U109* was probably sunk at this point.

Damant was not investigating U-boat wrecks around this time, as there were none to investigate. Instead, he worked on the wrecked tanker *O. B. Jennings* from March 26 to April 20, and then was ordered to the Admiralty.

PAPERS FROM *UB58*

In March, as is now known, several submarines hit mines, and the first of them was *UB58* under Löwe, out from Zeebrugge on the 9th. Early the next morning, after a patrol lit a flare to illuminate a line of drifters, a surfaced submarine rapidly dived. Almost at once, drifters and the patrol boat *P24* felt a series of underwater shocks near the Varne Light Vessel. At daybreak *P24* found a thick patch of oil containing bits of wood, loaves of fresh bread, and pieces of paper. The torn papers now in the Public Record Office -- perhaps the top third of each sheet -- came from the "Weight Report for Trimming Trials" of *UB58* on August 1, 1917, with mention of an 8.8-cm. deck gun, and the "Dockyard Trimming Trials" the same day at the A. G. Weser yard in Bremen.[247] There could be no question that *UB58* had been sunk. Hall told Sims that the U-boat was "evidently nearly blown to pieces, as they got her log book among the wreckage." By "log book" he meant these papers, but his conclusion was right. There was no reason to send down divers at the time, especially in a mined area.

APRIL IN THE STRAITS: THE WRECK OF *UB33*

The drifter *Ocean Roamer* observed another explosion near the Varne watch buoy on the late afternoon of April 11 and was able to pick up a bucketful of oil and some wood covered with an acid-proof composition. The location was not quite in the minefield, but it was thought that perhaps a submarine had fouled a mine cable and later ran into the mine. Two weeks after the explosion sweepers located a wreck, and on May 6 divers identified it as a submarine. At this point the Admiralty sent for Damant. He had already used explosive charges in the *Laurentic*, and he believed they would work here. Within two days he had applied to Curtis & Harvey for gelignite so that he could cut steel at twenty fathoms, but they told him that it contained less nitro-glycerine than before the war and advised the use of blasting gelatine. He then asked the Director of Naval Engineering for a permit to obtain three hundred pounds of this explosive but was told a week later that it was not available and he should try a substitute.[248]

When he reached Dover on May 21 he went down with Cdr. Cooper and a party from the Admiralty salvage tug *Moonfleet*. (This was a 100-foot steel vessel of 145 tons, built at Millwall in 1917.[249]) They found "a UB-boat, extensively damaged aft and lying on her starboard beam ends." About a hundred and eighty square feet of plating had been crushed. The body of an officer (*UB33's* commander, Gregor) was removed from the conning tower. Like many other smallish UB-boats, this one had an eye painted on the bow for good luck. "A mine lies on the sea bottom touching the damaged part of boat; it has at least five horns, one being doubled up. The number 832 is painted on the mine. It is a spherical mine" -- evidently British.

Four days later Damant was able to explode 45 pounds of TNT inside the conning tower (on the 22nd Sims was told about bodies taken from the conning-tower), and the next day used another charge to get into the control room. On May 29 Diver Miller, working with "the greatest energy and determination," finally got beyond the control room and recovered "material which appears to be of the highest importance" -- a steel chest containing signal books, ciphers, and related documents. Among them were the new call signs in effect from April 12 onward. Nothing like this had turned up since the salving of *UC44* eight months earlier. Cdr. Cooper took the box from Dover to London at once.[250] Miller's achievement was so important that in July the head of the Salvage Section requested a decoration for him,[251] and it was awarded the next year.[252] Many years later a local diver has described the wreck as "half buried in the Varne Bank." with conning tower detached.[253]

LATER IN APRIL: *UB55*

A second U-boat sunk during April was *UB55*, which Wenninger took out from Flanders on the evening of the 21st as the last boat to sail before the famous British raid on Zeebrugge and Ostend. She remained on the surface until her commander made out a line of eight watchers not far north of the Varne shoal. Soon after he reached periscope depth the stern of *UB55* fouled two mines and a violent explosion followed. On the bottom in thirty meters, the boat gradually filled with water. Twenty men managed to escape from the forward torpedo hatch and the conning tower, though many surfaced too rapidly and did not survive. About two hours later, drifters which had heard the explosion picked up the six who were still swimming. By June 21 Wenninger was able to send a letter from prison camp to indicate that "apparently on way out near Varne Bank hit deep mines."[254] Three months later he got a letter through Rotterdam to say he had hit a "double mine" at eleven meters. Along with this he sent a detailed report with many reliable details on what he had learned about U-boat sinkings during his interrogation. Divers found the wreck of *UB55* in August but by then it had no special value. In was found again in recent years.[255]

EAST COAST IN MAY

The small *UB16*, ordinarily an outpost boat off Zeebrugge, crossed to the British East Coast on May 6 and was southeast of Orfordness on the late afternoon of the 10th when *E34* chased her for nearly half an hour before firing two torpedoes. One hit the bow and did not explode but the other blew up under the conning tower. Ten minutes later one of the four or five men on deck was still swimming.[256] He turned out to be Von der Lühe, the captain, who was "badly shaken up and will not give any details at present."[257] A young officer who escorted him to London "made good use of the opportunity for conversation."[258]

The next day sweepers were already searching for the wreck when Damant was summoned from Portsmouth, where he was waiting for explosives. "Stand by to proceed with party to Harwich, for examination only, depth 13 fathoms, question of *Moonfleet* being sent being decided." *Moonfleet* soon arrived, and after a week the sweepers discovered something unidentified. Their wire slipped and when Damant went down all he could find, in "no visibility," was a piece of plating and some piping. It looked as if *UB16* had disintegrated when hit by the torpedo.

WRECKS OFF FLAMBOROUGH HEAD

On the night of May 31 *UC75* (W. Schmitz) found herself in the midst of a convoy off Flamborough Head and finally succumbed to ramming. At first sweeping for the wreck proved unsuccessful,[259] but on June 5 the Admiral at Immingham informed Hall that "further papers salved from German submarine *UC75* are being forwarded by tonight, Wednesday's, post." Something must have turned up, presumably of slight importance if sent by post.[260]

On June 7 air bubbles coming to the surface in the vicinity of *UC75* pointed to the presence of another wreck, and divers were able to locate *UC39*, sunk sixteen months earlier. Her wreck was so old that it did not justify a detailed investigation.[261] Any documents of value had already been recovered.

LYME BAY IN MAY

Whereas nothing was now being found in Straits and East Coast U-boat wrecks, an important Channel sinking took place on the evening of May 26. The armed yacht *Lorna* was escorting a convoy south of Portland at the eastern end of Lyme Bay when she sighted a periscope only thirty yards away. Since it was turned away from her to watch an approaching ship she was able to approach to ten feet before it dipped. *Lorna* passed over the spot and dropped one depth charge set to fifty feet, then another. Amid the turbulence four objects could be sighted and cries of "Kamerad!" and "Help!" heard. Determined to destroy the U-boat, she dropped one more depth charge and killed three swimmers outright before picking up the fourth along with a cap marked *Unterseeboots Abteilung*.

The survivor, who died after three hours, stated that the submarine was *UB74*, a week out from port, which had sunk three ships. In Germany Von Georg of *U101* later reported a meeting west of Ushant on May 25, when Steindorff of *UB74* told him he had sunk a steamer. This must have been *John G. McCullough*, sunk off the Ile d'Yeu on the 18th.[262] Given the probable date and place, *UB74* was the submarine attacked by the American yacht *Christabel* in the same area on May 21. Oil came up after a depth charge was dropped, and damage may have been at least moderate.[263] The basic fault was not in the hull, however, but in Steindorff's watch keeping after he had torpedoed a steamer off Portland Bill and then, eager to attack another, failed to observe the approach of *Lorna*.

Early in June a local diver in Lyme Bay found *UB74* lying on an even keel in twenty-one fathoms. The upper lid of the conning tower was open, as had been expected, and she carried a deck gun, "apparently 5.9 inches." The depth charges had made a tear three inches wide and forty feet long on the "port side extending aft from the torpedo tube." Cdr. Cooper, representing the DNI, gave orders not to attempt salvage but to try "to open the forward hatch into the officers quarters by means of explosives [gelignite]." On June 6 divers got in but found nothing but corpses and two small tin boxes with signal cartridges. A diver got in. He could not penetrate from the officers' quarters into the control room.

Hall was eager to hear of further results. He was weekending at Milton Abbey near Blandford in Dorset and told Intelligence officers to bring him anything found between June 14 and 16. Nothing turned up, however. By the end of the month the divers used explosives to demolish the conning tower, and a periscope (eye piece missing) was sent to London along with various small items. Hall himself visited Portland on July 1. Three days later a small package of documents was sent up to the Admiralty, but though divers continued to clear the wreck for nearly another month they found nothing more of value. Bad weather hindered their work, and entry into the control and radio rooms proved impossible. The Salvage Officer at Portland noted that at twenty fathoms "gelignite does not do the work." On August 11 the 10.5-cm. deck gun was brought up, and work finally ended on September 3.[264] (*UB74* was reinvestigated more recently.[265])

The documents found included lists of the crew of *UB74* for various dates in late 1917 and early 1918[266] and the Diving Log Book for November to May. *UB74* had passed through the Straits on the 12th, been rammed by a steamer off Beachy Head on the 13th, and missed a steamer (*Egbet*) with a torpedo on the 14th. The Diving Log Book ends at May 16. One earlier event could be checked, for the steamer that accidentally rammed her was *Nidd*, which felt "a heavy blow under No. 2 hold" and suffered heavy damage to the starboard otter, afoul of something that looked like a radio aerial. Since the U-boat appeared on the surface fifteen minutes later, however, her inner hull was intact. This haul of documents did not amount to much.

At the beginning of September the Rear-Admiral Portland asked Lt. R. H. Davis, who had been working on *UB74*, to "verify the sinking of a submarine by sending Mr. Miller down" seventeen miles west of Portland Bill in twenty-five fathoms. He said that the wreck had been located and buoyed. Salvage immediately refused, stating that "new case is not to be inspected." By then Miller, under Damant's orders, was busy with the more important wreck of *UB109* off Folkestone.[267]

FRUITLESS EAST COAST SEARCHES IN JUNE

On June 12 another U-boat was reported "sunk or badly damaged" off Flamborough Head, and Damant went to look for the wreck. In five days he found nothing, and on the 19th the Director of Naval Engineering wrote that

Commander Damant and party should not be sent to search for submarines as they are intended solely to be used after a submarine has been located and properly buoyed.

Three days later Damant was searching off the mouth of the Humber and found that a "fresh obstruction" was a rock.

EAST COAST: FINDING *UC11*

On June 26 Damant and his party were ordered to Harwich to search for a boat with much better prospects.[268] *UC11* under Utke had left Zeebrugge on June 24 to lay mines near the Sunk Light Vessel.[269] On the morning of the 26th she was at fifteen meters about a mile and a half from the Light Vessel and after a violent explosion she rapidly filled with water and dropped to the bottom. Utke managed to open the conning tower hatch and get out. The Light Vessel's crew observed the explosion and sent out a boat which after half an hour managed to pick him up. He said he was the engineer of a submarine which had already laid her mines but revised his story after the wreck was found.

On June 28 divers found the wreck of *UC11*, lying on its port side with a big break twenty feet abaft the conning tower. Though all the mines were still in their chutes, Damant proposed to open up the conning tower with explosives, and the DNI telephoned his approval of the scheme. The submarine belonged to the earliest class of minelayers and nothing was to be learned from the wreck as such. A hundred pounds of TNT were set off inside the conning tower, but the mines did not explode. Since entrance to the hull was still blocked, boats and personnel were got clear and another charge was detonated. This time "very large explosions" took place as mines went off down below. "Large quantity of debris floated up including important material which was salved." By "important material" Damant meant documents like ciphers. More "important material" turned up in the control room. He concluded that "most violent explosions can take place within a few feet of papers without destroying them,"[270] and acted on this supposition when using explosives in the Straits of Dover later in July.

What had caused the loss of *UC11*? The divers found two old German mines nearby and thus confirmed the opinion that Utke ran on to one of the mines that *UC11* herself had laid in either September or January, some months before he took command. The Admiralty claim that they had been left there on purpose is convincing.

THE DOVER STRAITS IN JUNE: *UC64*

Early in June continuing problems with the Dover Barrage forced Keyes to tell the Secretary of the Admiralty that the field was "getting very thin in places, especially between the Colbart and Gris-Nez "because many mines had broken adrift."[271] In spite of occasional encounters with U-boats, nothing decisive took place in the Straits until 0415 on June 20. At that time the drifter *Ocean Roamer*, on watch between Buoys 15 and 16 of the barrage, between the Colbart and the Varne, heard a heavy explosion and sighted a dark object under water. It was exuding oil and air and seemed to be heading northeast. Depth charges from *Ocean Roamer* and *Loyal Friend* brought up more oil and air for about seven hours.

The Admiralty urged Keyes to confirm the June 20 sinking. "When weather permits diver should endeavour to locate and identify wreck of submarine ... if this has not already been done." Keyes was naturally eager to prove the success of his barrage. On June 29 he complained that "I can't get several thousand pounds due to the Auxiliary Patrol for murdered submarines because I can't get a diver on to the submarines to identify them -- since they are in the minefield."[272] Around the same time he showed the American captains Knox and Yarnell, inspecting his operations at Dover, his chart with twenty-two "practically certain" sinkings, of which "a number" (he did not say what it was) had been located by divers.[273] Presumably with Keyes's complaints in mind, the Admiralty informed Sims on July 8 that five U-boats were known to be on the bottom of the Dover Straits. The figure was conservative, but "efforts [were] being made to raise or visit the interior" of the latest wreck.

On July 3 Damant arrived at Dover from Harwich, where he had been working with *Moonfleet* on *UC11*, and two days later, working at twenty-two fathoms, found a minelayer with mines in all six chutes and with torpedoes without warheads secured near the two deck tubes. The submarine had obviously been sunk on her way out through the barrage. Damant also reported a 22-pounder gun forward of the conning tower, camouflage painting, and a bottom coating that was "bran new and glossy, colour black or dark red." The conning tower hatch was "partly raised but immoveable," though he thought the closed hatches fore and aft might be opened. He regarded the prospects of getting papers as not good "on account of mines" -- referring to the German mines, though the divers also saw "one British mine lying on the bottom near her apparently waterlogged." During the next few days they got into the forward living compartment, "under which original explosion took place." Smashed wreckage came to within a few inches of the deck and had to be moved by hand.

> Between conning tower and mine chambers bottom of submarine is blown up ten feet so that fore living compartment is packed solid with debris of accumulator in which are embedded bodies in hammocks. Diver lies on upper deck and reaches down to throw out debris in handfuls. This process will take weeks. Only means of accelerating is to use explosives.

Hall agreed and wrote Salvage that "explosives must be used." The Salvage Department vetoed the scheme, however, because of the mines still in the chutes. In a letter of August 12 on the investigation of *UB74*, Damant himself noted how dangerous explosives were. "The risk of comparatively small charges detonating the torpedoes, etc., in the wreck is considerable. If my diving boat had not been veered well clear before firing on two occasions when this happened she would certainly have been sunk."[274] The wreck has been found again in recent years and identified (again) as *UC64*.[275]

TWO MORE WRECKS IN THE STRAITS

On July 14 Damant found another wreck, not far from *UC64*. "A small UB-boat, one gun, single screw, eye painted on bow, severe damage from mine explosion, evidently has been sunk some months, marine growth on parts sent up by diver." The "single screw" points to the class *UB1/17* (UB-I), but those boats had no deck gun, and none of them was sunk in the

Straits. The wreck must have belonged to the UB-II class, and was probably *UB38*. This submarine was sunk on the evening of February 8 when the drifter *Gowan II*, near the north end of Le Colbart, sighted her in a distant trawler's flare just before she dived, and twenty minutes later was shaken by a triple explosion, not far from a position where fuel oil came up to the surface for two days. Divers did not go down in the minefield, but prisoners picked up from other submarines gave the number of this one (*UB38*) to British interrogators. The wreck was found July 14 but not identified. Recently local divers have found the wreck again and McCartney has probably identified it as *UB38*.[276]

The next day, during a search for another U-boat supposedly sunk five days earlier and much closer to Dover, "a submarine was found, extensively damaged aft, with weed and marine growth on her, evidently not a very recent case. She was only located at the end of slack water, so time did not admit of a detailed examination being made."[277] The location and circumstances suggest that she was *UB31*, which had undergone depth charge attack on the morning of May 2 while trying to get eastward near the Varne. Oil and bubbles came up. This wreck too was not identified until recently -- from markings on propellers.[278]

BACK TO *UC64*

Part of the delay in opening 4 was due to bad weather, but beginning on July 16 Damant used small explosive charges to blow off the conning tower and enlarge the passage down into the control room. The divers did not reach their goal until August 1, when they found some "personal articles" to forward to the DNI "for identification purposes." What this meant was a purse found in the pocket of a man wedged in the debris. Because of the original mine explosion the floor of the control room was so badly forced up that entrance to the radio room was impossible. The submarine was *UC64*, out from Zeebrugge under O/L Schwartz only thirty-two hours before she hit the mines.

FIVE MORE WRECKS IN THE STRAITS

Meanwhile Damant was searching for U-boats in the Straits of Dover. On August 7 he was on the bottom in eighteen fathoms, two and a half miles North, one fourth East of Gris Nez, when he found "a UC-boat with two screws and two rudders, much damaged by mine explosion under gun, crushed and folded in neighbourhood of officers quarters." He could not tell whether her mines had been laid or not. "No body visible in the conning tower, and nothing by which to identify boat." Damant believed she had struck ordinary contact mines, even though the wreck was not far from the electrically controlled mines off Gris Nez. Though U-boat wrecks can move considerable distances on the bottom,[280] no submarine was mined electrically off Gris Nez except *UB59*, which survived the explosion. In any case, the wreck of *UB26* had yielded a list of resting spots on the bottom that included a location two and a quarter miles north-northeast of the Gris Nez lighthouse with a fine sandy bottom in 15 1/2 fathoms.[281] Perhaps the UC-boat was looking for that area, where mines had presumably been laid.

There are only three possibilities for identification among the larger UC-boats lost in or near the Straits during 1918. The first is *UC50*, lost in January, the second *UC79*, lost in April, and the third is *UC78*, lost in May. All that the British Museum of Natural History could say about barnacles on "a piece of tin" from the wreck was that the boat was sunk before June. Perhaps *UC50* would be too old, and *UC78* is an unlikely choice because of the location. U-boats stopped passing close to Gris Nez after *UB59* was damaged on May 3 and the radio station at Bruges warned U-boats that "off Cape Gris Nez are deep anchored mines." *UC78* had left Ostend on May 2 to lay mines off Boulogne and Newhaven and then operate in the central and eastern Channel. Seven German mines appeared off Boulogne on the 4th, followed by seven more off Newhaven on the 8th. Presumably she received the signal from Bruges and did not try to return near Gris Nez. Perhaps she could have caused minefield explosions noticed not far from the Varne on May 11 (twice) or two days later, though no wreck was found. In any event, she was almost certainly the submarine that attacked the troop transport *Queen Alexandra* off Cherbourg on May 9, and was rammed and sunk.[282] Thus the wreck is not *UC78* and not likely to be *UC50*, but may be *UC79*. The Admiralty decided against further examination and it was never identified.

On August 9 Damant found two more wrecks off the Varne near No. 13 Buoy.[283] The second U-boat had run into the first and lost its bows. Divers from *Moonfleet* the next day noted that "forepart of vessel as far as gun has been blown off by an internal explosion." The next day they "explored fore part of wreck up to control room bulkhead which is shattered." Inside they "found everything blown into small pieces, only fragments of bodies. Bedding and clothing rotten and fell to pieces when handled. No chance of anything important [documents] remaining...." On the 12th they were able to bring up the 10.5-cm. gun with its mounting. Previously they had found "bits of what appear to be high explosive, resembling lyddite," and one piece, presumably not very dangerous, was sent up to the Admiralty. Many years later the persistence of diver Dave Batchelor resulted in examining the boat's propellers. Since they were stamped "*UB58*" no further identification question remained.[284]

Damant in *Moonfleet* found yet another old wreck near this one on August 12 and described it as "a UB-boat which appeared to have been sunk several months... with no means of identifying her." The stern was blown in and the boat was nearly full of sand. The location, however, identifies the boat as *UB56*.

Two days later Damant found the wreck of a UB-boat "apparently with four bow tubes" approximately where *UB55* had been sunk, and two days after that fired an explosive charge "to enlarge the fore hatch." A heavy explosion followed, probably caused by the bow torpedoes. After a few days more, papers and keys found on a man wearing a leather suit were sent up to the Admiralty. Next the submarine's 8.8-cm. deck gun was brought up, and finally, on the 22nd, some books were forwarded to London. When Hall received the papers and keys he stopped the search and wrote to Keyes, "From an ink impression on one of the scraps of paper forwarded, the submarine has been identified as *UB55*....This is confirmed by an entry in the note-book recovered subsequently and sent up yesterday by hand." Since *UB55* had been sunk four months earlier the wreck could not provide fresh information. It was still "in good condition" eighty-five years later.[285]

EAST COAST: *UB110*

Early in the afternoon of July 19 *UB110* was sunk south of Hartlepool, Yorkshire. This new boat had arrived at Ostend from Germany only on June 27 and left Zeebrugge on July 4th, with orders to return after twelve days of operations against traffic in the East Coast War Channel. Meetings with *UC70* on the 18th and *UB77* on the morning of the 19th proved she was still afloat then, but no further news reached Bruges until August 2, when the Red Cross reported that the captain, the watch officer, and some of the crew were prisoners.

After meeting *UB77*, *UB110* was on the surface northeast of Whitby when an American plane piloted by Ensign J.J. Schieffelin bombed her as she dived, apparently damaging her diving rudders.[286] Three hours later she was under water south of Hartlepool and approaching a convoy. After her torpedo missed the French steamer *Yolande* a motor launch sighted the periscope only fifty yards away and dropped a depth charge, followed by four more from the escort destroyer *Garry*. The U-boat's diving rudders jammed in the up position; her port motor short-circuited, and a fuel tank was damaged. She came to the surface exuding oil, only to be rammed twice by the destroyer and hit with several bursts of gunfire. With her upper works torn open, the U-boat rolled over and sank. Many of the crew escaped but only thirteen were picked up. Some of *Garry's* stokers came on deck with large lumps of coal, throwing them at men in the water. Her commander, W. Fürbringer, added that stokers fired revolvers at them.[287]

The last entry in the hydrophone log of the submarine began with "12.55 pm. Noise of screws to starboard" and ended with "till" and a scrawled "2" written considerably lower. Presumably the battle began at this point.[288]

On July 29 Cdr. Wheeler located the wreck of this "large coastal submarine" northeast of Saltburn Pier, where oil was steadily flowing to the surface. The next day divers examined her in 26 fathoms, noted that her bottom was painted a "dirty green", and attached a buoy to her bow. A diver who landed on the deck saw that the gun had been "carried away" and that the conning tower was smashed nearby. A round hatchway with a 2-foot diameter was open. Cdr. Royle telephoned further details to London. The U-boat had been "rammed on the port side just abreast of the gun and just before the conning tower", so that the gun was pushed off its mounting.

> She has been rammed again aft the starboard side, the destroyer passing over her, but I do not think this has done more than crush the hull. She has had a depth charge underneath her forward, which has probably pushed her up, and she has had one shot through the conning tower casing on the fore side and another shot right through both the inner and outer hulls in the conning tower on the after side. Both upper and lower conning tower hatches were open.

Wheeler and his diving party suspended operations for searches elsewhere until they could return on August 10 and examine UB110 once more on the 15th. The decision had now been made to raise the wreck and tow it to Newcastle, and the towing began on September 19. Three days later, after German signals recalled U-boats from the American coast, the DNI sent instructions to shorten the time in dry dock, since a German attack might now be expected.

Investigation and search work inside the vessel, except as required to make her float, is not to take place at once as the object being aimed at is to first of all repair the hull damage without delay so that the floating dock will be available for Grand Fleet

emergency purposes.

The wreck reached Swan-Hunters Shipyard at Newcastle on October 4 and was immediately opened up for investigation. The First Sea Lord sent a telegram of congratulations, and a month later Hall contributed two hundred pounds. At last there was a rich haul of documents, including code books, ciphers, and radio logs. An especially important item was the *Allgemeines Funkspruchbuch* (AFB), "General Radio Book." The version from UB110 is complete, including Tauschtafeln or conversion tables for the ciphers Gamma Alpha, Gamma Ulli (U-boats), Gamma G[amma], and Gamma O[micron] for the supreme command.[289]

THE WRECK OF UB107

According to Gibson and Prendergast, relying on Admiralty reports, off Whitby another new submarine, UB107 (Prittwitz und Gaffron), "was depth-charged out of existence by the armed yacht Vanessa and three trawlers, on the 27th [July]."[290] Spindler expresses doubts about this report, noting an attack that sank two steamers about two hours later in a convoy in 5352/0010E. Since this cannot be ascribed to any boat but UB107,[291] he concludes that UB107 cannot have been sunk by Vanessa.

Spindler was certainly right, since the U-boat's wreck lies many miles away and must have been sunk under different circumstances. She was sunk by some unknown cause one mile north of Flamborough Head at position 5408N/0000W between July 28 and August 3, 1918. In recent years divers discovered the wreck, identified by markings on the propeller shafts, under the remains of the steamer Malvina, which was torpedoed and sunk by UB104 on August 3, 1918.[292] The sinking could have been accidental or caused by a British mine.[293]

THE LAST ZEPPELIN WRECK

On August 5 the Zeppelin L70, with the Chief of Airships Fregettenkapitän Strasser aboard, was shot down by a two experienced airship-hunters in a DH 4 two-seater. The wreckage fell into ten fathoms of water about forty miles northeast of Yarmouth. Two days later Strasser's successor informed the German Naval Staff that "one can assume complete destruction and that [classified documents] are not in enemy hands."[294] At that moment they were not in enemy hands, for Cdr. Royle was waiting for fair weather before undertaking salvage operations.[295] A week later, however, Hall was able to circulate English translations of the orders of L70 for her last flight, adding that the Chief of Airships had been on board), as well as a secret German document analysing Zeppelin losses.[296] (Robinson suggests that Strasser was working on the latter document when L70 was ready to fly and took it with him.[297]) Combing for wreckage went on for a long time, apparently without the discovery of a codebook. On September 22 Immingham telegraphed the Admiralty: "Admiralty Constructor reports that he has finished with the Zeppelin wreckage.... Request I may be informed whether the large quantity of wreckage may be taken to sea and thrown overboard as the space occupied is urgently needed for other purposes."[298] L70 was almost the last Zeppelin to fly over the British Isles in wartime.[299]

EAST COAST: UB30

Another U-boat sunk off the East Coast was the relatively old and small UB30 under Stier. She had already suffered damage from a bomb dropped at Bruges on March 24 and in spite of repairs tended to leak oil.

Out on April 29, she returned only two days later because of this problem. On cruise in July she again leaked oil after a depth charge attack and had to return to Zeebrugge. Her sinking was not due to leakage, however.

As early as July 29 an Admiralty telegram to the Rear-Admiral East Coast ordered him to send a C-class submarine on patrol until August 2 east of Flamborough Head where, according to information from UB110, U-boats were accustomed to charge their batteries. Though the C-class submarine sank nothing, patrols and convoy escorts were especially watchful after UB30's last signal, made at the northern end of Route 3 out of Zeebrugge at 0410 on August 7, openly reported, "Have started journey to the north." The Admiralty quickly informed Immingham that "Enemy submarine call sign WHE from Flanders can arrive in the latitude of Flamborough Head tonight, possibly to operate in Flamborough to Tyne area."[300] From the 8th through the 12th of August patrols off Whitby incessantly attacked the submarine. At noon on the 13th the armed trawler *John Gillman*, on watch as a convoy passed Whitby, sighted a periscope only three hundred yards away. Stier was looking at the convoy, three and a half miles distant. The trawler missed ramming the periscope by about three feet but at once began a vigorous attack by dropping two depth charges set to explode at a hundred feet, then circling round for two more at eighty. After an interval, oil and air came up. A little later the steam yacht *Miranda II* also dropped charges.

Two hours after the first encounter the trawlers *John Brooker* and *Viola* were keeping hydrophone watch when they sighted the submarine coming to the surface. Each of them fired two rounds at it, followed by five depth charges set at a hundred feet. Ten minutes later another trawler, *Florio*, arrived on the scene and immediately sighted the submarine close by, emitting oil and air bubbles as Stier tried to reach the surface. *Florio* and *John Gillman* finished off the U-boat with four depth charges set at a hundred feet and two at a hundred and fifty. All that came up was oil and air.

After the sinking of UB30 divers under Cdr. Wheeler were sent to the location off Whitby. An Admiralty Salvage telegram tells the end of the tale. "Submarine sunk on 13th August near L Buoy was today Saturday [August 17] located by divers in 27 1/2 fathoms LWOS. Unable to obtain her number." The prospects of recovering anything of value were minimal, and work was suspended in favour of the more important wreck of UB110.

Nearly eighty years later a notice on the Web, dated 25th August 1994, stated that a Whitby diver had been asphyxiated when his air ran out at around 50 metres depth, "on a recently discovered World War I German U-boat" where there was "an official German war grave."[301] A Royal Lifeboat letter to Captain A. B. Sainsbury (April 12, 1996) stated that the wreck was that of UB30.

UB20 OFF ZEEBRUGGE

On July 28 O/L Glimpf took *UB20* out from Zeebrugge for four hours of diving trials. He did not return but probably struck a mine Many years later the wreck was discovered, lying at 30 meters in 5121/0238E and positively identified from markings on the starboard propeller.[302]

DIVERS AND THE SINKING OF *UB103*

On the evening of August 14 Paul Hundius took *UB103* out from Zeebrugge, intending to pass close to Gris Nez on his way to Biscay. Four days later Bruges radioed him that he had been awarded the important order Pour le Mérite. There is reason to suppose he was already dead, however, for on the evening of August 15 the yacht *James Fletcher* and the drifter *J. Burn* were on patrol between Buoys 19 and 20 when the yacht sighted a periscope and attacked with depth charges. The drifter assisted with one depth charge which in turn set off two mines. The only U-boat in the Straits was *UB103*, presumably sunk at this time. Miller arrived but he too was unable to find anything

Later it was claimed that *UB103* was depth-charged off Gris Nez on the afternoon of September 16 after the dirigible *Z1* observed oil and air bubbles and summoned patrols. Oil did come up from this location. It is unlikely, however, that *UB103* survived so late. Hundius was an able and aggressive captain, and the fact that no sinkings or even attacks can be ascribed to his submarine suggests that he did not get through the Straits of Dover. Other U-boats could find targets around this time. More important, the notion that he was sunk as late as September 16 is not tenable, as Spindler intimated.[303] Hundius' orders told him to return "at latest after eighteen days,"[304] and each of his two previous cruises had lasted nineteen days. By September 16 he would have been two full weeks overdue. In addition, by that date U-boats were no longer using the Straits route but going north of the British Isles.

Finally, on September 18 "the position was thoroughly searched...but no indications of a submarine were found."[305] The Admiralty survey on minefields mistakenly states that "during further search *UB103* was located."[306] A drifter with electrical "searcher gear" did investigate an area a mile square around the Gris Nez position but found nothing.

After the Armistice the Admiralty had to reconsider the loss of *UB103* because on December 11 the captain of the drifter patrol at Dover claimed that this submarine, by now known to have been sunk, had been downed on August 15. They had already decided, however, to award a thousand pounds to the crews taking part off Gris Nez in September, and on January 4, 1919, the Secretary of the Admiralty informed Keyes of the decision. He questioned the conclusion twice, writing London on January 21 and 26, but the Admiralty could not be moved. "*UB103* is correct. Sailed

August 14 but not sunk until the middle of September when on her homeward journey." In the spring of 1919, further searches for U-boats lost off Gris Nez brought no results. Damant reported on April 8 that on twelve days divers had sighted nothing but "three or four mines riding to their moorings and the usual great quantities of electric cable." Admiral Dampier agreed with him that the search should be abandoned.[307]

THE LAST STRAITS SINKING: *UB109* OFF FOLKESTONE

The last submarine to be sunk in the Straits of Dover was therefore *UB109*, which encountered shore-controlled mines off Folkestone. Under Ramien she had left Zeebrugge at 0100 on July 28, heading first to the buoy off Blankenberghe, next at 285 degrees for eighteen miles or three hours, then lying on the bottom in 29 beta off Bligh Bank for the rest of that day, and finally aiming for Buoy 15 in the Dover barrage. There she was attacked about 2200 by the drifter *Monarda*, which dropped four depth charges on her track as she dived; two other drifters dropped five more. When the after hydroplane motor had short-circuited, the U-boat came to the surface. The crew were rushed forward to force the bow down, and she then touched bottom. The explosions she heard above came from depth charges though Ramien thought they might come from mines. After cruising near the Azores to investigate convoy routes, she headed back, sinking one small steamer four hundred miles NNE of the islands. Planes bombed her off Guernsey without effect, and she was able to sink two French vessels in the Channel, a total of 6375 tons for the cruise.

West of Folkestone the radio operator made his last entry in the radio log. "29.8.18 0312 [German time] Dived" as she headed for the Folkestone Gate. An hour later hydrophones on shore picked up her motors and in seventeen minutes the indicator showed that she was over a line of shore-controlled mines, which blew up under the engine room. As the U-boat dropped to the bottom about twenty survivors escaped through the conning tower and the forward hatch, but only the commander and seven others could swim until rescue craft arrived.[308] The next day Ramien wrote from a London prison to tell his father that "with the last three notices of 3000, 1000, and 4000 marks my property should increase to 150,000 marks."[309] What he meant was that his latest sinkings added up to 8,000 tons and brought his total to 150,000 tons. Even if one includes sinkings due to mines he laid in 1916 and 1917, however, the total was just over a hundred thousand.

Damant and company arrived at Folkestone soon after the sinking of the submarine, and *Moonfleet* left Dover early so that the divers could find and buoy the wreck by 10.30 the next morning. Keyes transmitted Damant's report to Salvage.

Diver got down through fore hatch cleared bedding and body from man quarters and got through bulkhead into forepart of officers quarters expect to be able to search them thoroughly. There is no damage to this part of boat but she is cut nearly in half at a point about 25 feet abaft conning tower. The prospects finding something are good. There is no need for explosives.[310]

Damant's own report was much the same.

Severe damage abaft engine room, no damage seen on fore side of conning tower, depth about 12 fathoms. Am sending a notebook recovered from coat pocket. Will dive next tide. Shall not use explosives without orders.

Progress was made the next day.

Obtained material this morning and forwarded to Admiralty. Work cut short this afternoon by weather. Obtained a little more material. Dived, reached Captain's room. Time is taken in passing contorted bodies up through narrow hatch to make room to work but I should expect success in 1 or 2 days of fine weather if material is not hidden.

On August 31 success was achieved. "Divers have reached fore bulkhead of control room and will be able to pass through. Recovered much material. Only able to dive one tide owing to weather." The day after that also brought results. "Got through control room into wireless cabinet and recovered much material. Bad weather prevented diving on 2nd tide." More papers turned up on September 3 and 4, but on the latter date Damant commented that "very few papers if any now remain."[311]

The daily briefings of Admiral Sims show something of what was being found. On the morning of August 31 he was told that "so far a chart has been obtained, showing the cruise of this vessel from the Channel to the Azores, then south of Gibraltar and up along the coast of Spain and France, and back into the Channel." In fact the chart showed that the circle cruise was taken in the opposite direction.

Apparently this was an exploring cruise to obtain information as to the track of convoys, several of which are written on the chart. It has not yet been studied, having only just been received. [This explains the error noted.] Other charts were also obtained which contained very important information.[312]

Had these papers been acquired earlier in the war they would have been priceless, but now, with the Germans abandoning passage through the Straits and, within the month, the Flanders base itself, they were not very useful. It was of value to have both the old edition and the new edition of the charts for navigation on the Belgian coast, but it was too late for much action based on information from them. *UB109's* library of code and cipher books was extensive, but the contents were largely known. It showed the trend in German cryptography, but this could change at any time. A cryptographer's dream had come true but too late. The Germans themselves were keeping careful count of the documents aboard U-boats that might be sunk in shallow waters. They were preparing to alter all their call signs in September and introduce new ciphers immediately thereafter. The value of the haul from *UB109*, like that of the hauls from *UC70* and *UB110* off the East Coast, was to prove chiefly historical.[313]

On September 4, as Damant seemed to be reaching the end of his "important material," he asked the Admiralty if wireless instruments should be brought up. Their answer was negative. They wanted him to concentrate on ammunition instead, presumably mindful of the Straits wreck whose bows had been blown off by an internal explosion. On the 16th they informed him that "*UB109* entrance to magazine is under control room on the fore part on the port side immediately outside W. C." He does not seem to have found anything significant, however, before being ordered north to *UC70*. On the 25th the divers received a telegram. "Cdr. Damant should be informed that diving operations on all wrecks are to be suspended for the present as he is required for new case off Whitby."

CONTROVERSY OVER DAMANT'S RESULTS

A Salvage list of August 28 aroused Damant's ire because it failed to give credit for much of his work. It mentioned wrecks numbered from 100 (*UB74*) to 110 (*UB55*) with credit divided among Davis (*UB74*), Wheeler (*UB110*, *UB30*, British *C12*), and himself. Though busy with *UB109* Damant took time to note the omission of nine wrecks he had dealt with, sending back his own list on September 5. "We have actually dived on 13 submarines."[314]

EAST COAST: THE DISCOVERY OF *UC70*

On August 28 another U-boat perished off the coast, this time *UC70* off Whitby.[315] Though the circumstances were quite different from those of *UB30*, the setting was rather similar, for August 1918 was notable for calm seas and good visibility. In July Dobberstein had taken *UC70* to Flamborough Head and had undergone fairly severe depth charge attacks. On August 19 he left Zeebrugge again but had to return for minor repairs. A Zeebrugge signal on the evening of the 20th stated that he had "proceeded out to make trimming trials off the Mole and will then proceed farther out." First he was to lay mines on the convoy route between Holland and England, then head for the East Coast. His activities during the following week are hard to trace, partly because another submarine was also working off Whitby. It appears, however, that UC70 was the boat whose periscope was sighted by a patrol plane around noon on the 27th. Two 230-pound bombs seemed to detonate close to the submarine and result in large amounts of oil and bubbles. Intelligence conservatively estimated that she was "possibly slightly damaged."

The next day, after UC70 torpedoed a steamer east of Kettleness, trawlers dropped depth charges, and about three hours later the patrol plane BK 9983, protecting a passing convoy, sighted an oil slick close in shore and then observed a submarine lying on the bottom. The plane immediately dropped a 520-pound bomb, and it "detonated about thirty feet from her starboard bow." Oil and bubbles came up, and the destroyer *Ouse*, despatched from the convoy, dropped seven or eight depth charges very close to the spot.

The wreck of this U-boat took more than a week to find, but on September 6 a diver coming up from his search bore smudges of light grey paint that turned out to have come from the hull of a U-boat. By the 9th he had recovered parts of the wireless gear and other pieces. A plate on the superstructure bore the words BERLIN FRIED[e]NAU. For the moment the wreck could not be raised because of the effort being made to salve UB110 and it was decided to wait for Damant to come from the south after he finished work on UB109 off Folkestone.

Damant finally arrived at Whitby from Dover on October 2, and soon asked Salvage for a small writing table with lock up drawers (for "secret documents") and a small typewriter. Further correspondence ensued; the typewriter arrived on the 18th, and a letter on the 28th informed Damant that "table will be supplied."[316] He left for Scapa the next day.

By October 8 he had found the U-boat wreck listing seventy degrees to port, with the fore hatch, conning tower hatch, and engine room hatch open. No mines were in the chutes. From the conning tower he extracted the body of an officer. "He was wearing no uniform but merely two suits of underclothes marked Dobberstein and a leather suit, all pockets were empty and he looked like an officer who had made his preparations for escape." The same conclusion could be drawn from the other open hatches, through which, at some point, crew members had tried to escape. In August a prisoner from UB110 had claimed that Dobberstein was "a most brutal officer and very much disliked by the crew." Within a few days Damant could partly explain this claim after bringing up several heavily locked iron cases. They contained not the secret documents he expected but, instead, sausages and tinned food. "Even a canvas bag containing potatoes was locked." The next day a diver was able to go in through the fore hatch and bring up seven rounds of 8.8-cm. ammunition.

On the 11th two divers got through to the radio cabinet and took out logs and several instruments, since Hall had given Damant specific instructions to get them. "Two bodies blocking the entrance were carried out and passed up the hatch; when attaching weights to one of these for sinking it was noticed that his throat had been cut." The divers offered no explanation.

Three days later they finally found the signal books and sent them to Hall, and the next day the search was over, since no more books could be found. "The supposition is advanced that in all probability same were destroyed by crew." A letter bearing the address *UC70* confirmed the identification already made from the commander's name.

Damant's report bears this annotation: "Read with interest and admiration. W. R. Hall. 20.X.18 DNI." Damant kept investigating the wreck even though later results were trivial, and left the scene only toward the end of October when *UB116* was unexpectedly mined in the Scapa Flow defences and he rushed north to investigate.

At Bruges there was concern about the loss of *UC70* not only because of a crew and boat but also because the British might have recovered secret documents. An official list from Bruges names eight secret documents on board,[317] at least three of which are to be found in the Public Record Office today. One is the *Allgemeines Funkspruchbuch* (AFB), with various *Tauschtafeln* such as Gamma Alpha with variants E, F, and G, Gamma Ulli 4th edition, good from August 11 to October 21, Gamma Gamma, and Gamma Beta. The book appears to have been wet along the edges. Then there is the *Funk-Namenliste*, with mud and water stains on the outside.[318]

Most of a sheaf of radio signals is somewhat torn, with mud and water on some, water on others. They come from the end of May 1918. The 13th item includes a drawing of a death's head in a long robe, riding on a torpedo with a red warhead and carrying a long spear. In addition, a list of the officers and crew of *UC70* in a notebook names Loch, Dobberstein's predecessor, as commander.[319] There must have been more documents, for a British description of her last cruise says that she "heard depth charges" on August 25 and 27. Only a logbook taken from the wreck could provide such information.

EAST COAST: THE SEARCHES FOR *UB115*

Early on the afternoon of September 29 the Scandinavian convoy was about to meet its escort off Sunderland when the dirigible *R29* observed oil coming to the surface and dropped a 230-pound bomb to mark the position.[320] The destroyers *Ouse* and *Star* proceeded to drop depth charges until more oil and air bubbles came up and three armed trawlers joined in.

U11 was mined off Zeebrugge in December 1914. It wasn't until another eighty years had passed that the wreck was found and identified.

Torpedo loading onto a UC-II Class minelayer at Zeebrugge.

Having run aground, UC5 was captured intact and paraded around Britain and America to raise war-bonds and aid in recruitment.

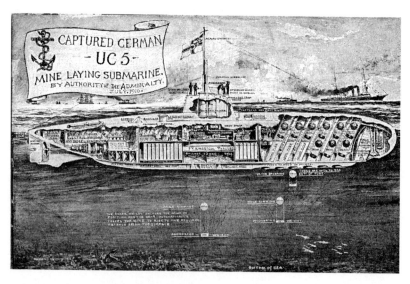

A souvenir postcard of UC5. Although her crew had released her mines, they were held in place during her salvage by using steel nets.

UB77 successfully experimented with radio position fixing in February 1918. She is seen here with HMS Victory as a war-prize in 1919.

View from the airship R29 of the attack on UB115 off Sunderland on 29th September 1918.

Lohs, the aggressive commander of UB57. His body, and those of some of his crew were washed ashore. One had a bullet wound in the head. The loss of UB57 has never been explained, nor the wreck found.

Loading mines into a UC-II Class minelayer. When released, they dropped out beneath the submarine. The deployment of minelayers in dangerous shallow waters partly accounts for their high loss rate.

U151 seen from the American SS Pinar del Rio, shortly before it was sunk by the U-boat, on June 8th 1918. Its heavy armament is clearly visible.

Business in great waters – A U-Cruiser stops a British steamer.

The U-Cruiser U155 after surrender in 1918

Q-Ship and quarry. HMS Suffolk Coast on display with U155 in St Catherine's dock in 1918.

The U-Cruiser U139 at sea. Note the damaged conning tower.

The presence of the armoured cruiser HMS Bacchante off Sierra Leone could do little to prevent panic upon the arrival of the U-Cruisers in West African waters in 1918.

Hunters successful! – U126's British crew in 1919. Note the gun behind. The U-Cruisers could deliver formidable firepower.

Lt-Cdr. G. C. C. Damant
who supervised at least 13
U-boat wreck investigations

Diver E. C. "Dusty" Miller
whose work on recovering
intelligence material from
sunken U-boats won him the
DSC and MBE.

Royal Navy divers in standard dress. Considerable courage and skill
was needed to investigate lost U-boats.

UB81's deck gun today. Bad weather interrupted diving on this wreck in February 1918. It was relocated by divers in the 1980s.

UB81's stern torpedo tube today.

(Photographs of the encounter were taken from the airship.) In spite of obvious damage the U-boat kept trying to surface on her motors until early evening, but nothing was heard later. Oil came up for the next two days, and on October 1 sweepers found an obstruction, presumably the wreck of *UB115*. Since the depth was twenty-eight fathoms, only salvage divers could investigate, and they were busy elsewhere on more productive cases. No result came from a "very thorough sweep" on October 29, and by the Armistice nothing had been examined. Captain James, speaking for the DNI, set forth the official view on January 24, 1919: "It is not considered that further operations are justified."[321]

The sinking has now been confirmed, however, and the wreck of *UB115* found in position 5514N/0023W, 4.5 miles northeast from Beacon Point, Newton-by-the-Sea, off Northumberland. "Up until ten years ago she was intact and complete, but is now broken into two sections, each standing about 3m high and lying on a 'spoil-ground' of the ash from the local power station," [which] sets like concrete. However "the wreck is covered in soft corals and most of her is still there and attached to the wreck which was probably destroyed by trawling."[322]

THE SINKING OF *UB116* IN SCAPA FLOW
Orders for Hans Joachim Emsmann were issued on October 23,

if possible during the night of October 28-29, otherwise that of October 29-30, to attack the British fleet of ships of the line in Scapa Flow, making every effort so as to weaken the enemy as much as possible before the decisive battle.

His route into the Flow was given in some detail.

The northerly route by Muckle Skerry seems easier for navigation. From there on, passing by Lothar Reef, keep close to the shore up to Hoxa Sound. In Hoxa Sound, according to the report of *UB126*, there is an illuminated area. Observation of October 17. There it will be necessary to cruise submerged.

A "special source" identified by Spindler as "incomplete reports on daily ship movements" added that only the western entrance to Scapa Flow (Hoy Sound) was mined, while Hoxa Sound contained neither nets nor mines.[323]

On the evening of October 25 Emsmann left Heligoland. The last notice in a notebook found aboard ran thus: "8.30. Proceeding with escort, course 310, Heligoland abeam."

On the afternoon of the 28th, watchers on South Ronaldsay sighted the submarine and alerted the British defences. Hydrophones at Scapa were immediately activated. "The course of her destruction was logged in the following manner by the Stanger Head operators," writes Hackmann.[324]

> At 2221 faint fast running engines heard and reported on Nos 1 & 2. At 2223 enquiry was made of EDO as to any expected vessels; to which negative reply was received. At 2235 same engines were reported to EDO as being motor engines and possibly those of a S/M. At 2236 searchlights were switched on to a position given by O-in-c, and engines were at once heard to stop. At 2258 very suspicious sounds of auxiliary engines -- probably S/M submerging -- heard. At 2304 S/M was heard practically over No. 2 instrument. At 2312 S/M passed through line of instruments, and was in Hoxa Sound. Warning was given to the Mine Magnetophone Station. From 2312 onwards S/M was apparently making straight for the Boom of Hoxa, and at 2330 was located over the magnetophone minefields. A line of Mines was then exploded, since when nothing suspicious was heard.

At daybreak oil and air bubbles were coming up in great quantities, and a depth charge brought up a German naval watch coat. That day Damant was working on *UC70* off Whitby when a priority telegram reached him.

> Proceed at once by rail to Scapa with two divers and equipment and necessary members of your party to investigate new important case. Report when you proceed and wire Vice Admiral, Longhope, when you are due Thurso so that quick sea passage can be arranged b him. Your vessel [*Moonfleet*] can be sent later if required.

Damant replied at two in the morning from the station at York. "By order Admiral, Immingham, am catching 0252 train from York but apparently cannot reach Thurso until 1355 on 31 October. Am taking two divers and wiring Admiral, Longhope, to arrange equipment." Eight hours later he had reached Edinburgh and wired again. "Arriving Inverness with men at 1622 today but cant reach Thurso until 1325 tomorrow unless special arrangements are made for transit. Please wire me any instructions c/o Stationmaster Inverness." Evidently the special arrangements were made, for that evening Damant informed London that the submarine had been lost and refound but the weather was too bad for surveying.

Divers had already visited the wreck but did little more than describe the conning tower. This led to a mistaken guess that the submarine belonged to "the *U63* type," mistaken because as the DNI noted "all are in the Mediterranean."[325]

On November 1 Damant reported some results.

Surveyed wreck today. Found hull to be completely shattered and collapsed from 10 feet abaft conning tower to within 20 feet of stem. There are several large tears through inner and outer skin and back is broken. Owing to damage prospects of recovering material are bad but have cleared away wreckage which was blocking fore hatch and will get a diver inside tomorrow Saturday to see if there is room to work. I do not consider there is enough longitudinal strength for boat to be lifted and position of minefield makes use of explosives undesirable. Have got out four bodies and handed material for identification boat to A[dmiral] C[ommanding] Orkneys and Shetlands. A few letters and a notebook are being sent to DID by Admiralty messenger tomorrow. From entry in notebook it appears *UB116* was at Heligoland s recently as Friday 25th Octr.

The notebook was the one already cited,[326] while the "material" Damant wanted consisted chiefly of ciphers -- none of which was recovered.
Since the notebook showed *UB116* at Heligoland on the 25th, she obviously had a "special task." If the Admiralty released news of her destruction, that would indicate that her position was known and that secret documents might have been recovered. "This is undesirable."[327]
A report sent to the German Navy by the Admiralty on October 10, 1919, describes what the divers found.

Three bodies were found by divers in the conning tower of the boat, but the pockets were all empty. Divers got down into the boat through the fore hatch and cleared the way aft through two compartments to the control room bulkhead. This was a matter of great difficulty, as the way was blocked by two torpedoes which had evidently been slung up on Weston's purchases ready to reload the tubes. There were also several bodies and many kit bags packed with new, clean clothing and assorted literature.

It proved impossible to get into the control room.

After some days work one of the divers reached the control room bulkhead. The door was partly off its hinges and jammed. After digging away the bedding and debris from round the door he found the forearms and hands of a man thrust through the crack at the lower part of the door seating, but who this was cannot be known as no more of him than the arms to the elbows could be reached. His body was the other side of the jammed door in the collapsed and inaccessible control room.[328]

On the 5th Damant was informed that if *UB116* were to be raised, Cdr. Wheeler, in charge of salving *UB110*, would take over and he himself would assist. His specialty after all was searching submarines, not raising them. On the 13th, however, after the 10.5-cm. gun was brought up the Admiralty stated that "salvage of *UB116* has been permanently abandoned." The Armistice had been signed, and the lines of mines in Hoxa Sound were to be re-laid only at the local admiral's discretion.

By this time the officers' quarters had been entered but there was no documentation except for "personal material." Indeed, a diver who worked inside the boat reported that "debris and pieces found give the impression that a torpedo has exploded internally."[329]

II

AREAS OF ACTION

We have already seen results from interception in encounters around the British Isles and in the German Bight, but the most dramatic results occurred when the large cruiser submarines arranged meetings off the African and Spanish coasts or announced impending arrivals in the North Sea.

8.   U-CRUISERS TO THE SOUTH

RENDEZVOUS OF *U156* AND *U157*

When Germany badly needed wolfram ore for tungsten in July 1917,[330] Prince Ratibor, the German ambassador to Madrid, proposed to ship it from Spain. The logical choice of a carrier was one or more of the *Deutschland* class of big commercial U-boats recently converted to military service.

Deutschland herself (now *U155*) had visited America twice as a cargo-carrier and like her sisters was too slow and clumsy for active warfare in the North Atlantic.

Discussions between the Admiralty Staff in Berlin and von Krohn, the naval attaché in Madrid, were conducted by radio from Nauen in the VB code and ciphers thought to be secure. Both the French and the British could read them, however. The *Scientific American* for October 11, 1919, contains a picturesque story of how they overcame the "Nauen-Madrid buzz" by May 1916. Madrid would buzz for five to twenty seconds and Nauen would buzz back. The Allies were recording all this meaningless noise on cylinders, when a wind-up record player ran down and the sounds became distinct. Listeners deduced that "at Nauen and Madrid each message was cut into a perforated roll" which was "run through the sending apparatus at the speed of 400 words per minute." The story may be roughly correct, but Paris had been reading the signals since July 1915. Indeed, there was a special centre at Bordeaux for listening to Madrid communications and by the end of the war the French had intercepted thirty-three million words, including comments that led to the execution of Mata Hari.[331]

In the summer of 1917 the British were gathering their own information from watchers near the French border at San Sebastian by the end of August and at Bilbao in September, where the British agent Maurice Mitchell reported on the 15th that there were fifty tons of wolfram.[332] The Germans were moving rapidly, and on October 2 Berlin asked von Krohn about shipping the ore by submarine from the Canaries perhaps in November. On the 16th he stated his preference for the Bay of Biscay. The only U-cruiser immediately available was the newly commissioned *U156*, which could easily accommodate some tons of wolfram. Precisely on the 16th, however, she had sailed under Gansser for "U-cruiser war in the North Atlantic." On the second and third days out, torpedoes from British patrol submarines missed her, while on the fourth day severe storms off the Norwegian coast brought water into the control room. On the 24th she announced her return. "Have broken off my undertaking. Rapid vacuum installation No. 5 jammed. Leakage of water on diving.... Propose to be at Kullen Light House on Friday at 2200."[234] Gansser reached Kiel after a twelve-day cruise which accomplished nothing and did not facilitate the transport of wolfram.

Von Krohn meanwhile arranged for a sailing vessel out of Bilbao that could meet a U-boat in early December. After Mitchell informed London that the wolfram was being loaded into fifty-pound sacks, Hall telegraphed Gibraltar to "use every endeavour to prevent wolfram from leaving."

On November 7 Berlin informed Madrid that two U-cruisers, *U156* and *U157*, could reach the Canaries on a certain date which the British could not decipher, perhaps "24 November." Each of the submarines would take on forty tons of ore. Whatever the date, the information impressed the Admiralty so forcibly that they immediately ordered two E-class submarines to proceed from Buncrana on Lough Swilly "to Gibraltar as soon as possible... for a special operation against enemy submarines in vicinity of Canary Islands for which orders will be sent to Gibraltar." *E35* sailed on the 10th, *E48* two days later.

On the 19th Madrid transmitted a description of the *Erri Bero*, the ship that was to carry the wolfram, and three days later the two British boats left Gibraltar for the Canaries, only to be recalled on the 27th when Berlin informed Madrid that the two U-cruisers would arrive only at Christmas, meeting at "U-Platz 130." Madrid had to inquire where U-Platz 130 was. London and Paris joined Madrid in waiting for the answer, soon forthcoming: the Platz lay on the southwest side of Ferro (Hierro) Island in the Canaries.

The stage was set and all that remained was for *Erri Bero* to load her cargo certified as cement, for the date to be made final, and for a trap to be sprung. On December 8 Madrid stated that "a safe time for the meeting would be from December 31." By the 12th Gansser had brought *U156* out again and was shelling Funchal, Madeira, in order to damage the cable station there. Just at this point the German plan became somewhat confused. Berlin told Madrid that the ship was to be "at the meeting place from January 20," only amplifying this message on January 3 with news that *U156* and *U157* would arrive at the rendezvous between January 15 and February 1. Both on the 3rd and the 5th, however, von Krohn reported that the ship had already sailed and could not be recalled.

In fact, *Erri Bero* had left Bilbao with the wolfram at 1830 on December 31, only to encounter the British auxiliary patrol *Duke of Clarence* shortly after midnight. A boarding party captured the ship with its crew of five Spaniards and one German, though while she was under tow to Plymouth she went down with the wolfram because of heavy seas or sabotage. Hall had the prisoners detained at Cromwell Gardens Barracks in London, and in February he wrote to the Spanish consul general. "Five Spanish seamen have been rescued ... from the Spanish schooner *Erri Bero* which subsequently sank... It is desired that they should be repatriated via France... Rear Admiral Hall begs to enclose a cheque for 50 pounds which he understands will cover the cost of their journey to Spain." One can imagine Hall's sardonic amusement as he wrote. The Germans reporting from Madrid ascribed confusion to the British. "The one sailing vessel according to news received was stopped by the English on her return journey, but before the sailing vessel had been searched she was sunk by her crew. The English appear to have been badly informed."

Relying on the German signals about the rendezvous between January 15 and February 1, the Admiralty now ordered Gibraltar to have four E-class submarines ready for the Canaries by the 10th. They were to proceed to Ferro and maintain a diving patrol during the last seventeen days of January. *E48* under Lt.Cdr. F.H. Taylor sailed on her mission on the evening of the 10th and arrived to investigate the U-Platz at dawn on January 14 before continuing on patrol for the next seventeen days. She thus reached her destination a day before *U156*.

On January 15, when Gansser reached the Bay of Naos on Ferro, he believed he was the first to arrive, and though he regarded it as a poor location, he spent two days overhauling his engines and then anchored off shore on the morning of the 17th. In his opinion no enemy submarine could surprise him there, especially after he had sent three officers to use a hill ashore as an observation post. In mid-afternoon they reached the top and began their watch.

Fifteen minutes later a lookout aboard *U156* spotted a periscope thicker than German types, three feet above the surface and only sixty yards off the bow. While the jolly boat hastened back to pick up the officers, the periscope appeared again, this time four hundred yards away. Gansser was finally raising anchor, though he had supposed that a British submarine would not attack him in Spanish waters.[335] He now thought the enemy had passed under his keel and might be getting ready to fire. His own boat shot at the periscope and it disappeared, and as he made for the open sea he nearly ran over the enemy submarine, which followed him under water but gradually fell back. After three quarters of an hour Gansser concluded that the enemy would remain out at sea and that he could safely return to pick up the officers on shore. Nearly an hour later he got them aboard and began to leave the area. Suddenly the British periscope appeared, a thousand yards away, and he could see the tracks of two torpedoes running toward him. Firing at the periscope again, he went full speed astern, and the torpedoes missed ahead by about three ship's lengths and then blew up on the shore. Another torpedo followed, several seconds later, suddenly turning to hit *U156* amidships. When it did not detonate but circled on the surface, the U-boat kept clear by going full speed ahead. Four sailors on deck who saw the torpedo jumped overboard; one of them was pulled back aboard, two swam ashore, and one drowned. The submarine herself suffered only a leak in a diving tank.

The next day Gansser radioed to *U157* : "U-Platz compromised, danger for U-boats." The German Admiralty Staff report later noted that he owed his escape to luck and criticized him for his "strong aversion to cruising submerged."[336] Gansser had other critics. A prisoner in British hands, perhaps not the most reliable of witnesses, called him "laziness personified" and claimed that "if his leg slipped off the sofa on which he was lying he would probably ring for his servant to put it back again." Valentiner of *U157* complained about his Bavarian accent but liked his good humor.[338] The Staff report did not discuss the danger incurred by using radio to arrange meetings for U-boats.

Before dawn on the 17th *E48* had dived north of the island and slowly worked round the west end. In mid-afternoon Taylor sighted a surfaced submarine four miles to the east, and half an hour later he was ready to fire at the target when the German vessel got under way and headed for him. He dived deep and escaped, then chased the U-boat off to the south, never closer than three thousand yards. When the enemy headed back and finally stopped, Taylor attacked with both bow torpedoes at seven hundred yards. The port torpedo broke surface but ran on. The starboard one jammed in the tube with propellers running. Taylor put his helm hard aport so he could fire from the stern tube. During the turn the starboard bow torpedo began its run and also broke surface. *E48* came up to fifteen feet and came under German fire. One more torpedo was ready.

> When the sights came on the stern tube was fired, the enemy then going about four knots. This torpedo also broke surface, ran slow, and apparently either went under or just missed astern -- range 900 yards. Stern torpedo was fired 2 minutes after the bow ones. Enemy proceeded to westward and chase was given, but abandoned when it was too dark to see through periscope.

Naval authorities in England were not enthusiastic about this report. On February 22 an angry Commodore (Submarines) S. S. Hall wrote that though "Taylor had sunk *U40* with *C24* and 100 fathoms of 3 1/2" wire trailing from his boat," and was an experienced and skilful commander, his record of the encounter was "the most unsatisfactory report I have ever had to deal with." Taylor and two officers had already been relieved. By March 9, however, Taylor was able to tell the enquiry that "it is possible that it [the stern torpedo] may have hit and not exploded." The DNI had evidently intervened, supplying the substance of a February 21 German signal with the news that *U156* had been struck amidships. Taylor was soon restored to command and took over another submarine by May.

U156 and *U157* made contact the day after the attack but constantly varied the cipher for fear of interception and decryption. The next morning they met southwest of the Canaries. Valentiner insisted the whole scheme had been betrayed but agreed to meet Gansser a hundred miles south of Ferro before the 23rd. A signal from Nauen also instructed *U157* to meet *U152*. At 1800 on the 20th, however, Valentiner told Gansser not to meet him. Since the weather was bad combined operations would have no point. He urged Gansser to follow his example by working with a prize steamer and not transmitting any more messages. He was convinced that the British could read them.[339] During his entire cruise of 135 days Valentiner sank only 10,000 tons, and on his return he was given sick leave. He was unable to walk after his endless cruise.[340] Gansser was relieved of his command.

British intelligence had turned this part of the "cruiser campaign" into a noteworthy failure and had shown how dangerous it was for U-cruisers to exchange signals, especially when arranging a rendezvous. U-boat captains who neglected this lesson would suffer fatal consequences.

THE SAGA OF *U153* AND *U154*

February 1918 orders for *U153* under Götting stated that she was to cut cables off southwest Ireland and along the African coast from Dakar. Both this submarine and *U154* under Gercke enjoyed modest success off the west coast of Africa during March and April. In March the British command at Gibraltar became aware that U-boats were operating off the Moroccan coast, and the destroyer *Celandine* began a search on March 12. The next afternoon the destroyer was on patrol when she sighted a periscope on the starboard beam and a torpedo missed her. An hour's intensive search, followed by three hours of cruising to the points of the compass, brought no results. *U154* did not report the encounter. In fact, Gercke never made long-distance signals that could locate him.[341]

Later in March the two boats met west of the Cape Verde Islands, where the two commanders decided to cut cables together, proceeding to the southwest of Orango Island, where two from Bathurst (near Dakar) crossed. The fishing operations resulted in nothing but the loss of lines and grapples.

On April 7 Gercke laid six mines off Freetown and then went down the coast toward Liberia, where German influence had been strong ever since the country was established in 1847 -- though a French radio station occupied a hilltop in Monrovia and Liberia had joined the Allies on August 4, 1917. At that time the German consul threatened that a U-boat would pay a visit, but he was not taken seriously.[342]

U154 arrived off Monrovia on the night of April 9-10 and sank the only Liberian government vessel at sea, an ex-German schooner of 100 tons. In the morning he sent a boat in to the capital with a message from "Herr Woermann" of the influential German shipping firm, and an ultimatum of his own.[343]

> I have not the wish to do unnecessary damage to the Liberian people, being sure that you were driven into the war against your will as well as against your true interests. Therefore I send you back those prisoners I made boarding your ship President. In the same time I want to draw your attention to the fact that the capital of Liberia is at present helpless under German guns. Like many other Allies of England and France you are not being supported by them in the moment of the most critical danger. If the Wireless and Cable Stations of Monrovia do not at once cease their work, I shall regret being obliged to open fire on them. If you wish to avoid this, you will have to send me a boat under a flag of truce and declare that you consent to stop them yourself.

President Howard could easily recognize the submarine's 5.9-inch guns but he consulted with his vice-president and some legislators before replying in a most formal manner. He repeated most of what Gercke had said and concluded, "I now beg to assure you that the necessary steps have been taken by me to stop all operations of the Wireless and Cable stations erected in this city."

Gercke understood the reply to mean that the Liberians would not comply with his demand but would not object if U154 destroyed the station. He sent another letter to the president.

> (1) The French flag is to be removed from its place shown to your commissioners. (2) Fire is to be set to all houses belonging to the Wireless and Cable Stations, the apparatus of each Station to be destroyed.

Both demands were to be met "within one hour after your commissioners have reached the shore."

Confused contemporary accounts tell a different story about Gercke's demands and reflect the popular mood in Monrovia. Rumor said that he asked for the surrender of all the Americans, British and French in Liberia, and that an unnamed British representative proposed to accede in order to spare either the lives and property of the inhabitants or the lives of women and children.[344] At two in the afternoon President Howard sought a compromise. He had given orders to lower the French flag, but asked that the radio and cable stations simply stop operating and be closed by the Liberian government "in the presence of the Netherlands consul." Gercke replied that he intended to destroy the station by gunfire.

According to Gercke's statement to Götting of *U153*, "shortly before the time expired the next morning, the government boat brings an accurate plan of the site of the radio station and consent to its destruction, which then followed." His memory played him false, for he bombarded the station not on the morning of the 11th but for an hour beginning at four on the afternoon of the 10th. The German *Postamt* found the news from Monrovia distressing, as *U154* might have destroyed the old German cable station instead of the French one. (Two months later they could be informed that neither one had really been destroyed.[345]) The British consul was able to use the cable, formerly German, to make his report to Freetown.

> Owing to refusal of Liberian government to burn and destroy French cable and wireless stations at Monrovia, German submarine 10th April sank Liberian defensively armed merchant vessels schooner and bombarded Monrovia for one hour from 1600 destroying wireless station. Casualties 3 children killed 3 persons wounded. All Europeans safe. Submarine ceased bombardment to attack steamer proceeding towards Sierra Leone. Both lost to view in dusk result of attack not known. Submarine announced intention resume bombardment today Thursday [11th] to destroy French cable station so no further messages will be received.

The steamer for Sierra Leone was the Elder-Dempster liner *Burutu*, carrying seventy-five tons of bullion as well as a hundred and ten passengers, a crew of ninety-five, and sixty-five laborers. *U154* went underwater to pursue, but after missing with a torpedo she "bounced up to the surface" to begin firing. *Burutu's* radio was shattered by the first of the U-boat's sixty or seventy shells. There was only one other hit but it opened the hull and resulted in a heavy list. One passenger was killed, two more and one pantryman wounded. A Kroo boy jumped overboard and drowned.

Burutu's gunners and their seventy-six shells saved the ship, as did the decision by her master, H. O. Yardley,

> to clear from the land, with the object of evading altogether the submarine; and estimating the chances, I felt sure he would look for me

towards the land, as, having the heavy list, he would think that I might have to beach the ship.

Heading out to sea, though with two boats riddled by shrapnel, he escaped after dark. By morning the submarine was gone, and Yardley was later awarded the DSC.[346]

When Liberia entered the war Hall had commented that "the action produces no naval advantage to us except perhaps the use of the W/T station." The British expected to provide defence from Sierra Leone, though it was not quite clear how. Occasional visits by the ancient cruiser *Bacchante* were not especially reassuring, even in London. Indeed, just two days before *U154* shelled Monrovia Hall noted that "some fast craft with at least 4-inch guns are required at Sierra Leone." A note in the files says that the submarine "*J1* has been ordered to Sierra Leone with the special service [decoy] collier *Bombala* to carry spares and fuel for her." But *J1* never sailed for Sierra Leone, and *Bombala*, out from Gibraltar on April 18 with the tug *John O Gaunt* in tow, never arrived there.

On April 25 *U153* and *U154* were more than a hundred miles west of Cap Blanc, far to the north of Dakar, and fifteen miles apart when Gercke radioed his position to Götting and added "See freighter WNW, 11 sea miles off, zigzag, generally southward." *U153* first dived, then came to the surface and opened fire on the freighter at ten thousand yards. The steamer kept on zigzagging as she turned to the northwest, shelled by both submarines but answering their fire. An explosion aboard *U154* brought her attack to an end but *U153* intensified her fire. Four boats, two lying very low in the water with many wounded, soon pulled away from the ship. As one of the boats came close by, *U154* also neared and the boat took the ship's doctor of *U153* across to her. A German shell had exploded on deck and left eight dead, five severely wounded. *U153* then came close to the burning freighter, which turned out to be *Bombala*, sighted her concealed 4-inch gun at the stern and others on each side, and sank her with a torpedo. The action had lasted two and a half hours.

Gibraltar picked up one radio message from *Bombala*, for in a brief summary record there is this note: "Reported attacked by two submarines at 1200 25th April in 2052 North 1736 West. No sign or news of ship." On May 10 the Senior Naval Officer Gibraltar telegraphed the Admiralty, perhaps because a signal was intercepted from *U153*. His telegram read thus: "Secret Can obtain no further information here with regard to SS *Bombala* have you any news of her." Nothing definite was learned until May 23, when Dakar sent a report from Leading Seaman J. Leadley, "who is, as far as is known here, the sole white survivor of this ship." Leadley confirmed that Bombala had made a signal.[347]

After their encounter with *Bombala* the two U-boats kept moving slowly northward. Neither the British nor the German command knew they were together, and no inferences seem to have been drawn from *Bombala's* signal about two submarines. Nauen signals of April 28 and May 4 announced the promotions of Götting and Gercke to Korvetten Kapitän. These signals were made separately and Cruiser Command seems to have had no thought that the submarines were cooperating. Another Nauen signal on May 6 instructed *U153* to patrol between the Azores, Madeira, and Gibraltar, while *U154* was to operate either north or south of the Canaries. Ernst Hashagen was on his way out to the Azores in *U62*, temporarily assigned to Cruiser Command. His orders, dated April 28, told him to make a rendezvous with *U153*, not *U154*. On May 7 Nauen told *U153* that Hashagen would arrive off the Azores in about three days and that she was to meet him, then patrol to the south while he operated off Gibraltar. In London the next day Hall informed the Americans that "a U-boat not cruiser was bound for the Azores and should arrive there about 10th inst."

On Thursday May 9 the Admiralty intercepted signals of crucial importance. At 0200 Götting reported his position in 3615 North, 1348 West, as well as the modest tonnage sunk by *U153* and *U154* on their cruises. "Besides this we have sunk in common in an artillery fight the English submarine trap *Bombala* of 3314 net registered tons." At 0250 he asked Hashagen for his position, course, and speed. Apparently the call sign was wrong and there was no reply, for two hours later Nauen intervened to give two correct call signs for *U62*, as well as information about her position, course, and speed the day before. "Call by radio; try to arrange a meeting." In conformity with this order Götting immediately gave Hashagen -- and the British -- the basic information that the rendezvous would be in 3645 North, 1200 West, west of Cape St. Vincent. A further Nauen signal told both cruisers to supply *U62* with torpedoes and fuel before the end of May.

At 1132 that morning an Admiralty telegram marked "Priority -- Clear the line" was sent to Gibraltar.

> Two enemy submarines are expected to meet about noon on 11th May in Lat 36 degrees 45 minutes N Long 12 degrees W or possibly farther to Westward on same parallel. Make every effort to send *J1* and *E35* to intercept them. After remaining in vicinity of rendezvous for 24 hours from noon on 11th May *E35* should cruise in Southern portion of Area 3 and J-1 should return to Gibraltar.

Gibraltar replied with a "secret" message: "Submarine *E35* can sail from Gibraltar evening 12th May [obviously too late]. Submarine *J1* should arrive noon 9th May."[348] It was certain that one boat would be there.

An hour later these submarines received their orders. Even though *J1* had just returned from a 17-day patrol, both boats sailed at 2030 on the evening of the 9th. The next night the last pieces of the puzzle fell into place. Hashagen informed Götting that he would reach the rendezvous at 1800 on the 11th, and Götting replied that he would be coming from the south in a scouting line ten miles from *U154*. This was the first mention of the latter boat.

Slightly to the southeast of the position, *J1* found the sea too rough for a patrol at periscope depth. She surfaced and spread canvas screens on the bridge and between the periscope standards to give the effect of a German conning tower.[349] No U-boat came by to judge the effect. *E35* under D'Oyly Hughes had better luck. On the 11th, after spending most of the morning and early afternoon under water (at one point he thought he saw a periscope or two nearby, but this must be wrong), at 1600 he sighted a "long low lying object ... about 2 to 3 miles distant."

Twenty minutes later he was sure it was an enemy submarine coming to the rendezvous from the southeast. *E35* altered course several times and was running roughly parallel to the target when it swung round and headed back because near the limit of the rendezvous area. Hughes quickly fired his beam torpedo at a point where "enemy's length was taking up almost the whole width of the periscope." His hydrophone operator could hear the torpedo run as it passed under the enemy. Evidently the Germans heard it too, for the U-boat altered course toward *E35* but passed directly ahead of her as she too swung round and fired two bow torpedoes, set at seven and a half feet, at the two German gun turrets. Both were hits.

The Starboard Torpedo made very little noise but threw up a large column of water and debris. The port torpedo did not appear to produce such a good burst but the noise and concussion felt in *E35* were very powerful indeed, the whole boat shaking and a few lights going out momentarily. When the smoke and water column had cleared away there was nothing to be seen but a quickly expanding calm area with some wreckage floating in it.

Hughes scanned the horizon, then surfaced to pick up three survivors clinging to wreckage.

I had the coxswain and one able seaman on deck with life lines, revolvers, etc., when Sub-lieutenant Summers arrived on deck and almost at once spotted another large submarine of the more usual U-boat type on the crest of a wave bearing 270 degrees distant about 2 1/2 miles.

E35 dived at once. The hydrophone operator thought he picked up "a torpedo getting louder and then fainter on the Starboard side." No German torpedo was involved, however, for Götting had only escape in view.

Hughes had sunk *U154* with Gercke, his crew, and the British Sub-Lieutenant Eric Allan, third officer of *Bombala*. In *U153* Götting sighted the boat four sea miles away as it vanished in a pillar of water and a dark cloud of smoke. After the lookout spotted a British submarine surfacing nearby and diving again several minutes later, the U-cruiser remained on the surface and headed southwest at top speed.[350] *U62*, late for the meeting, sighted the cloud on the horizon and soon received a warning signal from Götting.[351]

Hughes met *J1* the next afternoon and requested her to pass the news on to Gibraltar, since he was remaining on patrol. He remarked that "enemy was identical with photograph you and I saw in GSO's office except that this one had two circular turrets instead of open guns." *J1* bore the glad tidings back on May 14 and in London Admiral Sims heard them that day. Nauen kept sending instructions to all three U-boats until May 20, when the homeward bound *U153* reported to Cruiser Command that *U154* had been sunk by an enemy submarine on May 11. The next day the Admiralty informed the Northern Patrol that *U153* would "pass north of the Shetlands at any time between Noon 27th May and Noon 29th May and it is thought probable that she will cross the meridian of Greenwich between 6130 and 62 N, thence steering a course outside the 100 fathom line, at an average speed of about 130 miles a day, into the Kattegat."[352] No further contact was made with her, however, and on the 25th the Admiralty released the news about *U154*.

Hashagen, like Valentiner before him, believed that the British were reading the German cipher. He was told this was not likely, for directionals could have accounted for the presence of the British boat.[353] The Imperial Naval Cabinet noted the May losses of many U-boats, including *U154*, but hoped the rate of sinkings would decline because of fresh study of the operations methods of enemy submarines.[354] A study of the surprise attack on *U156* might have been more useful.

Back in Monrovia rumours were flying in June. A visit by the cruiser *Bacchante* did little to quell them. People said that Paris had fallen to the Germans, or that fifteen American transports full of troops had been sunk off the American coast, or that no more American troops were to be sent to Europe. On June 21 Hall offered a note of cheer. "It is suggested that in order to comfort the Liberian government, they might be told that the submarine which shelled the W/T station was sunk by the Navy on 11 May with all hands."[355]

9.   U-CRUISERS TO THE WEST

During 1917 Intelligence was aware that the Germans were building several new cruisers faster and more reliable than the seven converted merchantmen, since they obviously wanted to bring the war to the coasts of North and South America. Operations by such cruisers off the American coast seemed unlikely during the year, though the cruise of *U155* to the Azores raised such a possibility. A *New York Times* article on January 18, 1918, tried to allay public anxiety. Its heading ran "Naval experts see no likelihood of German submarines crossing Atlantic." The possible effect on morale seemed important to Americans and Germans alike. Thus Michelsen, BdU at the time, expressed his regret that "the small number of our cruisers did not let us hope to maintain the terror that their arrival was expected to arouse in America."[356]

THE FIRST VISITOR: *U151*

On April 18 *U151* under von Nostitz und Jänckendorff sailed for American waters. That day Nauen signalled her departure though not her destination, but further signals on April 22 and 27 discussed circumstances on the American coast. References to Bermuda and the Azores in the April 27 signal also led the Admiralty to suppose *U151* might take that route to America, but by May 1 detailed information was available and Sims was able to paraphrase the full text of signals to her for the Navy Department.[357] The very next day an American steamer exchanged gunfire with the U-boat and radioed her location, and the day after that *U151* reported her own position to Rugia. Obviously her raid would be no surprise.

The situation became even clearer on May 14, when Nauen sent instructions to lay mines off Chesapeake Bay and Delaware Bay. The next day as Sims transmitted the information to Washington he echoed Hall's requests and stated that

> there are circumstances which render it highly important that nothing whatever should be given out which would lead the enemy even to surmise that we have had any advance information concerning this submarine, even in the event of our sinking her, and that such measures as are taken by the department be taken as secretly as possible and without public disclosure of the specific reasons.[358]

As usual, the reference was to the secret of decryption.

The next day *U151* threw off what was left of her veil of secrecy and fired a torpedo that missed the British steamer *Huntress* by about six feet. The steamer's call to Bermuda gave away the position, a thousand miles east of Cape Hatteras, as Nauen informed her on the 21st. It also gave the Navy

Department the opportunity to issue an Alert. (The adventure of *Huntress* became public in the *New York Times* on June 1.)

U151 made three more attacks on shipping without success before getting down to business and depositing six mines in Chesapeake Bay on the 24th and eight more off Delaware Bay on the 27th. The only effect of any of the mines was damage to the tanker *Herbert L. Pratt* on June 3. On May 28 she was able to use her cutting device on two cables out of New York sixty miles southeast of Sandy Hook, one north to Canso, the other south to Colon.[359]

The U-boat's activities in American waters lasted for a month from about May 20. If we subtract three ships sunk on the homeward voyage, we find that she torpedoed one ship of 4588 tons and used gunfire or bombs to sink sixteen more of 31752 tons, a total of seventeen ships and 36340 tons. Presumably the only purpose of such a cruise, lasting ninety-four days in all, was to affect American morale and secure the recall of destroyers from European to American waters. Neither goal was achieved. There was a three-line headline in the *New York Times* on June 4: TWO U-BOATS SINK 9 SHIPS OFF THIS COAST; RAID BEGAN MAY 25, HEAVIEST LAST SUNDAY; CAROLINA MISSING; HOT PURSUIT BY NAVY. It thrilled the Kaiser,[360] but more important was the news that the New York stock market was "firm."

Another pinprick produced by *U151* was the capture of the Norwegian freighter *Vindeggan* on June 8. She was carrying 2500 tons of copper, and the ex-mercantile submarine busied herself for two days with taking on seventy-seven tons before sinking the steamer.

As she returned to Germany she encountered steamers nearly every day, and the Admiralty could estimate the date of her arrival off the Faeroe Islands and send out hunting patrols to find her. On June 28 Nauen ordered her to pass through Atlantic Quadrant 540 (with a centre in approximately 5115/2345) and the Admiralty concluded on July 7 that she had probably reached that quadrant. The Official History states that they "had information that a large cruiser submarine would be passing south of the Faeroes, homeward bound, on about July 12."[361] In fact, the operation against her was then delayed for 36 hours.[362] A brief memorandum by Hall shows how hopeless the hunt for this submarine was.

An enemy submarine converted mercantile type was estimated to pass 61 degrees N in about 6 degrees West [just south of the Faeroes] between midnight 12/13 and midnight 14/15 July. The Northern Patrol was informed that her surface cruising speed was 6 knots, submerged cruising speed 3 knots. From the position subsequently obtained by directionals, she appears to have passed about the time these hunts began, and to have maintained her surface cruising speed of 6 knots. It is therefore fair to assume that both hunts heard her to begin with.

Unfortunately, as he also noted, even though *Marksman* with four other destroyers, and five sloops with five trawler divisions, were on watch, the hunts took place in the wrong directions.[363] In addition, the positions obtained for *U151* on July 6 and 7 seem to have been off by about six degrees of longitude. Newbolt writes too optimistically that the hunters "presumably caused the U-boat commander and his crew great anxiety during the whole period."

Well to the south of the Faeroes on the 13th, *U151* did have some anxious moments when two torpedoes passed ahead of her as she went astern on both engines. On the 15th Nauen warned her of strong British patrols north of the Shetlands, but she was already nearing Norwegian waters. After eight hours there she was attacked by a British submarine again,[364] but reached Kiel on the 20th to a mixed reception. The public response was enthusiastic. "Boats came from Kiel with our flotilla chief and his entire staff to welcome us. One brought Prince Adalbert, son of the Kaiser." The Kaiser himself was less enthusiastic, probably aware of how little had been achieved.. At Spa, von Mueller

> had recommended him to receive ...the brilliant commander of *U151*, K/K von Nostitz und Jaenkendorff, who has just returned from a trip to the North American Coast. His Majesty refused on the plea that he must have rest and that his house was not a hotel, but later he somewhat surlily consented.[366]

U156

The orders of *U156*, now under Richard Feldt, took her like *U151* to the American coast. In case of bad weather farther south she was to operate in the Gulf of Maine at the end of July, while at the end of August she was to be off Halifax and cutting cables near Canso.

Her sailing on June 16 had been delayed because of an engine overhaul, and a signal made after eleven days at sea reported "frequent oil explosions because of pistons." She told Nauen, however, that she was able to proceed with the voyage. (Obviously she had suffered no significant damage on the 20th in a two and a half hour exchange of gunfire with two trawlers guarding fishing boats southeast of the Faeroes.) On July 1-3 the homeward-bound *U151* tried to make radio contact with her but received no answer. In mid-July Nauen calculated that she was now off the American coast and therefore transmitted information about American landmarks and coastal traffic. The message dealt with Cape May and Cape Hatteras, but about July 7 *U156* had changed course toward New York. In fact she was busy laying eight or nine mines off Fire Island, one of which sank the armoured cruiser *San Diego* on July 19, without loss of life.

A signal from Nauen that day listed gunfire targets. Munitions with thirty large cranes were to be found at Beachmont on Broad Sound (south of Revere, Massachusetts), while another dock and munitions depot, with a large electric crane, could be attacked near Portland on Casco Bay, as well as a shipyard at Newport on Narragansett Bay with two battleships under construction. Other targets lay on the New Jersey coast: a shipyard at Beach Haven, North Tucker Beach, a railway between Barnegat and Beach Haven, and a dock at Atlantic City that should be destroyed or damaged.[367]

It is not at all clear that the British read this signal immediately, or that it reached the U-boats addressed, or that the idea was practicable. It may have been related to Admiral von Holtzendorff's proposal for an official blockade of the American coast. The Kaiser rejected his proposal on the 13th, however, and sensibly informed him that "on the strength of what he already knew, he did not feel inclined to wage this war with a couple of submarines."[368]

On the morning of July 21 *U156* appeared out of a fog bank three miles off Orleans, Massachusetts, on the eastern shore of Cape Cod, and used her deck gun against a tug towing four coal barges, setting fire to the tug and sinking three of the barges. An American plane from the Chatham Naval Air Station soon circled over her, but without effect. It is hard to see why the submarine should have wasted even half of the 147 shells H. J. James says she fired at these targets.[369] The location may provide a clue, for at Orleans the direct cable from Brest, France, reaches shore. Since it was used for all the cable traffic between Washington and AEF headquarters in France, the U-boat probably grappled for it in the fog and then shelled the vessels that appeared over its location. Many years later "it was discovered that one of the barges had indeed landed on the cable without causing an immediate break."[370] (The barges were under tow off the east shore of the Cape because of the high tolls charged by the Cape Cod Canal, and after this episode the government took over the Canal and required coal barges to use it.)

The next morning the *Boston Globe* published a report telephoned by Dr. J. Danforth Taylor of East Boston, who from his cottage on a bluff overlooking the entrance to Nauset Harbour noticed the U-boat opening fire three or four miles offshore, and kept the phone line open for two hours while he watched the action. At one point he commented that "there is an 'airship' hovering over the fight, but it seems to be doing nothing but looking on." It was supposed to be an airplane from the station at Chatham. Another arrived after the U-boat had submerged and left the scene.

That day the submarine received a Nauen signal. "In case undertaking in the Gulf of Maine is influenced by foggy weather conditions *U156* is to operate off Delaware Bay." On the 27th and the 28th she may have been in

113

that area, where *U140* twice called her without making contact. Prisoners taken aboard from a sailing vessel she sank on August 2 were told, however, that she had waited for shipping three miles off Portland, Maine, but when none appeared proceeded to the Bay of Fundy. There she sank fishing vessels and a few steamers before capturing the Canadian sailing ship *Triumph* on August 20 and using her as a decoy to sink six schooners to the southwest of Canso. The British intercepted a plain-text German signal she made on the 23rd. It read "Why don't you give," presumably addressing the prize crew aboard *Triumph*. Probably -- as at Orleans -- the attacks on insignificant tonnage masked more important attempts to cut cables, this time off Canso.

Homeward bound on August 31, *U156* sighted the 5699-ton Naval Overseas Transportation ship *Westhaven* and opened fire on her. The transport replied vigorously and after twenty minutes the submarine gave up the attack. Three days later, long before dawn, she unsuccessfully shelled the British steamer *Alcinous*, and on September 6 she finally used her radio for a long-distance transmission. London read the signal: "Thus far /41 / thousand /tons / American armoured cruiser / San / Diego / P / 5 / cut / cable / position / 389 / middle."[371] Atlantic Quadrant 389 meant roughly 46 degrees N, 36 degrees W, the position of *U156* at the time. Michelsen thought that "P5 cut cable" meant she cut five cables, but the meaning is unclear. Conceivably it referred obliquely to the barges and the cable off Orleans. All could calculate that at seven knots she was now about a fortnight west of the Faeroes.

On the afternoon of the 7th, Cruiser Command sent orders about her route through the Northern Barrage. "Go round to the west of the new English mine barrier. Danger of mines in the eastern part and in Norwegian territorial waters." On the 10th her sister submarine *U152*, outward bound, received the same order about the route and then crossed northward by going up a line on approximately 2 degrees east longitude. That same evening, too late, a different advisory was radioed to her, with a supposedly safe route from northwest to southeast in the central minefield, recently discovered by *UB94*. (The chief of the Second Flotilla, to which *UB94* belonged, still preferred "the route west of the field," but this was not reported by radio.[372]) This second signal to *U152*, which *U156* presumably picked up, added confusion to the previous orders.

In addition, Feldt doubtless received a signal made by von Arnauld in the new cruiser *U139* reporting his position just east of the Shetlands on the 16th and stating that he had gone round "west of the barrage" at night. Such a route could be taken safely with the luck *U152* and *U139* had enjoyed, but any attempt to pass between the Orkneys and Fair Isle would have been highly dangerous in view of the mines laid there on September 7 and again on the 20th.

Since radio played such an important role in the homeward journey and sinking of *U156*, it is regrettable that we do not know exactly what went wrong. We do not know what signals the U-boat received between June 22 and September 10. A British captain aboard from August 11 to 16 reported of her 30-foot radio masts that "she used to put them up sometimes," but it is not clear that they did much good.[373] *U151* vainly tried to make radio contact with her on July 1, 2, and 3, as did *U140* on July 30. She does not seem to have received a Nauen signal of July 22 ordering her to Delaware Bay. Perhaps like some other submarines she could not use her radio for long-distance transmissions. This might explain the en clair signal of August 23, not received at home. Birch noted that *U156* was "apparently delayed on her homeward passage,"[374] but we do not know why. Engine trouble may have recurred.

On September 18 *U139* was north of St. Kilda and inquiring for *U156*. Two days later Feldt was close enough to make contact, informing *U139* that he lay to the southwest and asking for a route through the barrage. He also tried to report to his base about traffic conditions in the Atlantic and on the American coast, in spite of the obvious risk of interception. "Large troop transports proceed out and back alone on the shortest route. All others in convoy by no regular routes. Gulf of Maine no traffic, on the other hand much traffic Halifax--New York with protection." This signal corrected the description of traffic sent to him from Nauen on June 22.

U139 then requested a rendezvous. Making arrangements and finally coming together off Rockall took all day, chiefly it would appear because of problems with *U156's* radio and perhaps her out of date enciphering. When they met, von Arnauld must have advised Feldt that his own route west of the barrage, that is, just east of the Shetlands, was the safest. He knew nothing about new mines in the barrage and he had no reason to commend the route toward the southeast taken by *UB94*.

Feldt was not satisfied. On the evening of the 22nd he picked up a signal with the information that *U161* had passed northward through the barrage without incident, and at 1013 the next morning he made a recognition signal which *U161* answered twelve minutes later. At 1025 he gave his position and asked, "When and how did you pass round Skagen and the English barrage?" *U161* replied in Gamma Alpha cipher, which *U156* evidently could not read, probably because a new key had just gone into effect. (Similarly *U117*, also returning from a long cruise to America, signalled on September 20 that she had no Gamma Alpha key on board.) At 1115 *U161* cautiously asked the cruiser to "come within reach of visual signal." Apparently forgetful of British interception, *U156* referred to "lack of time" and asked for a report by radio. *U161* gave nothing away. "I was not at Skagen. The route is in accordance with Mine Signal 37." Since Mine Signal 37 had to do only with the Kattegat and in any event would be superseded by Signal 38 in two days' time, the answer had nothing to do with Feldt's most important question about the route. *U161* was in no position, however, to discuss her recent experiences by radio. She had tried to pass through what turned out to be the centre of the new field off the Orkneys, but after meeting several patrol destroyers on the 20th and mines the next day she had crossed farther to the east. What she could tell Feldt was useless.

The last act began on the evening of September 23 when, after receiving a report from *U139* that she had met *U156* three days earlier, the Chief of U-boats ordered *U156* to report her position -- not her proposed route -- and the date she expected to be picked up in the Kattegat. *U156* was now close enough to base for her to pick up this signal, and at 0200 on the 24th Feldt supplied information that was crucial not only to U-boat Command but also to British listeners.

He gave his position between the Faeroes and the Shetlands, and said he expected to reach Skagen no sooner than the evening of the 27th. In addition, he answered a question that had not been asked, explicitly reporting that he would pass through the middle of the barrage on the 25th from grid Quadrant 1660 to 2014. This was the mine free track followed by *UB94* on August 27[375] and proposed for *U152* on September 10. The BdU did not reply for fourteen hours but then imposed some restrictions.

> Proceed by the proposed route only by day and in calm weather. Keep good lookout for glass balls which carry mines. Report time of arrival at Skagen when south of the new barrage. At 0200 reception according to mine signal Rugia.

The signals of Feldt and the BdU thus gave the precise location and the approximate time when *U156* could be expected north of the barrage.

After the British intercepted the signal from *U156* and read it in record time, the destroyer leader *Marksman* was immediately recalled from sea to stand by for special duty. With the BdU signal in hand, the Admiralty sent a telegram to the Submarine Officer of the Northern Patrol.

> Homeward bound enemy submarine cruiser will pass latitude 59 degrees 56 minutes N., longitude 1 degree 30 minutes E., between daylight and dark tomorrow September 25th. If Submarine *L8* can reach this position by daylight she should be sent leaving patrol for base after dark on 25th.

Marksman met *L8* off Kirkwall, Orkney, and escorted her past Shetland toward the waiting place.

At 0745 on the 25th the British submarine was on the surface when she "sighted vessel nature undistinguishable" and dived at once. The undistinguishable vessel also dived, for nothing could be seen through the periscope, nor anything heard on hydrophones. An hour later L8 came to the surface and spent the rest of the day patrolling the waters to the north and south. Lt. Cdr. T. Kerr, her commander, later judged that the "vessel sighted was a submarine as no mast or funnels were showing. She was visible intermittently only. It is thought that we were seen also and that she dived at about the same time."[376]

Feldt's state of mind when he spotted a British submarine can be imagined. He certainly did not expect to meet one in this part of the North Sea, and he realized that the British had read his signals. His first officer, J. Knöckel, had been serving in U156 when radio interception led to the attack by E48, and all aboard were aware that Ul54 had been ambushed and sunk at a rendezvous. The atmosphere must have been tense. The last order Feldt had received had stated that the U-boat was to take the proposed route only in calm weather, but the sea was already getting rough. If he surfaced in the vicinity he would probably encounter L8 again; and if there was a submarine at the northwest end of the route there might well be another to the southeast. Passage under water could be even more dangerous. What was he to do? It now appears, thanks to the research of C.-H. Ankarberg, that Feldt decided to maintain his course, and four or five hours later struck the antenna of a mine laid to the southeast on July 30. His U-boat is probably an "unknown non-dangerous wreck" lying at 110 metres in 594415/015600E.[377] In view of the experiences of other U-cruisers, it remains odd that he had used radio to describe his route so clearly. His signal was not responsible for the destruction of U156, but it helped explain what happened.

Signals ordering U156 to report her anticipated time of arrival at Skagen were picked up on the 26th and the 27th, and Hall took pleasure in telling Sims at the morning briefing on the 28th that "it was expected that U-156 would report approaching port yesterday. She has not been heard from. It is consequently thought that she is in difficulties." By October 7 the Chief of U-boats had to admit she had been sunk, but four days later the order went out not to publish a death notice for Feldt, since his command was presumably known to the enemy. This expression of caution came rather late in the day.

TWO LESS SUCCESSFUL RAIDERS

A Nauen signal of August 8 stated that U152 (Franz) and U155 (Eckelmann) would sail for the American coast in mid-August and lay mines east of Atlantic City and Currituck, also off St. Johns, Newfoundland, and Halifax, Nova Scotia. On September 14 the Admiralty informed the North American Command that a "converted mercantile type of submarine ...is expected to mine the entrance of Saint Johns and western entrance of Halifax and to operate between Cape Race and Halifax."[378] After learning of mines laid off Halifax (by *U155*), Hall gave Sims the position of *U152* from signals made on the 18th and 19th, and since she was evidently bound for the waters off New Jersey the patrols there were alerted. When Sims heard of the alert he warned Washington again about secrecy. The Admiralty were perturbed, he said.

Their experience in obtaining and handling highly secret enemy information has involved serious difficulties and dangers. Entirely apart from the danger of jeopardising the source of information there is also involved the safety of agents.

The wording must come from Hall, who always insisted that interception had to remain secret.

The chief claim to fame of *U155* was that on September 17-18 she laid mines off Halifax, where they were found two and a half miles from the Sambro Bank Light Vessel before they did any damage. She did not carry out her orders to lay mines off St. Johns, Newfoundland, and her only other achievement was to cut the Canso-New York cable on the 20th. At the beginning of August she had been practising cutting cables in Kiel Bay and evidently mastered the technique. On October 11 both she and *U152* were ordered back to the Azores. In imperial circles it was believed that "the Foreign Office has recalled our U-boat cruisers (two ancient vessels) from the American coast to spare the feelings of the American nation."[379]

Some officers evidently regarded cable cutting favourably, for the cruiser submarines and a few others were regularly engaged in this task. Both officers commanding submarines, Bauer and his successor as BdU, Michelsen, considered it a waste of time and effort. Bauer noted that the cables had to be cut near the coast and could be repaired without difficulty.[380] Michelsen pointed out that the task diverted submarines from their true mission. Indeed, for the work to be successful many cables had to be cut "simultaneously and permanently." He knew of only one successful venture, that of Feldt in *U156*, who cut five cables on the North American coast and reported his success by radio.[381] Feldt may not have cut five cables, and other commanders had cut them too, but Michelsen's conclusion was certainly right.

U152 never reached Atlantic City but, though hit by a steamer's shell on September 24 with the consequent loss of 13,000 litres of oil, conducted a vigorous war on shipping in mid-Atlantic. North of the Azores on the 29th she chased the American tanker *George C. Henry* and in two hours fired 116 shells at her,[382] while the tanker replied with fifty-seven.. The range was too great for conclusive results, even though a hit near *Henry's* gun aft blew up its magazine. The fire aboard ship lasted for forty-five minutes but an effective smoke screen concealed the situation from the U-boat. An American naval officer stated that "we were well within his range, his latest shots either exploding or dropping into the sea close alongside." *Henry's* speed of thirteen knots, however, enabled her to escape from the slow ex-mercantile boat.[383]

At dawn the next morning the watch officer of *U152* sighted a nearby steamer on an eastward course, laggard from an 18-ship convoy. It was too late to dive as the steamer turned toward the U-boat, which manned her guns and opened fire. The steamer replied but a German shell set fire to the bridge and killed several officers, while further shells riddled the steamer's hull at the waterline. In the distance Franz could see an approaching escort cruiser and he submerged, surfacing later to finish off his prey. In all, he fired 83 shells. The vessel was the U. S. Navy transport *Ticonderoga* (5130 tons) with troops and munitions for France. Losses were heavy: ten naval officers, 102 sailors, two Army officers, and 99 soldiers.[384]

U152 used her guns expertly but fired no torpedoes, laid no mines, and cut no cables. She had expected to sail in mid-August but her commander and chief engineer had been suddenly relieved, perhaps because unwilling to make a cruise in an "antique." Franz took command only on August 29, a week before sailing. In light of these circumstances, the 6876 tons he sank represent a considerable achievement.

ASSESSMENT OF THE MERCANTILE "CRUISERS"

The operations of the ex-mercantile submarine cruisers were essentially a waste of time and effort. Even *U151* achieved little off the American coast, and the results of the other boats were inconsequential. Sinkings off the African coast had been equally insignificant. Radio interception drastically hindered attempts to coordinate operations, and two of the older cruisers were lost with all hands.

These boats were constructed because German authorities wrongly supposed that America would not enter the war. They were converted into warships apparently to avoid waste, although they were already obsolete. They were employed in waters far distant from the centre of the naval war and could have sunk only a small percentage of the tonnage needed for victory. They used men and materials that could better have been employed elsewhere.

THE NEW CRUISERS

At the end of January 1918 the American Naval Planning Section in London produced a memorandum on new cruiser submarines. In addition to the ex-*Deutschlands*, Germany was going to have twelve real cruisers, the first to be in service by August. By then all the cruisers would probably move to the western Atlantic in order to "interfere with American support to the Allies."

If the new cruisers came on the scene they could be formidable. They were to displace 1930 tons on the surface, 2483 submerged. They were more than three hundred feet long, with four bow tubes for nineteen 50-cm. torpedoes and two 5.9-inch deck guns. Their powerful engines had more than four times the horsepower of the *Deutschlands* and could drive the boats at 17.7 knots. When they dived -- in thirty seconds -- they would rely on electric motors twice as powerful as the older ones.

Counter-measures were possible. Above all, "the maximum possible effort should be made to destroy the enemy cruiser-submarine when it leaves or returns to its base." (This item was obviously based on British experience.) The other items, not evidently presented in logical sequence, included convoy, destroyers, hunting groups, heavier armament for merchant ships, longer range radio equipment, land stations directing shipping at sea, and hunting groups of submarines. Presumably under British influence, the memorandum stated that no destroyers could be sent back to America from European waters.[385]

A LARGE NEW MINELAYER TO AMERICA

Since the new cruisers *U140* and *U139* were long delayed, the impressive but untested new minelayer *U117* (1164/1512 tons) sailed for American waters on July 11, reaching home on September 22. Her captain, Dröscher, was an expert in minelaying who earlier commanded medium-sized minelayers. During his 74-day cruise he fired nine torpedoes (four hits), used 207 of his 624 shells, and laid thirty-three mines, but he sank only 20,654 tons of shipping.

When Dröscher got back the BdU explained that he had been sent to America to attack shipping. His own understanding was that the main task had been to lay mines. He had laid nine off Barnegat, seven off Fenwick, eight off Winter Quarter, and nine south of Currituck, all between the 13th and the 16th of August. Though a Fenwick mine damaged the American battleship *Minnesota* on September 29, there were few other results. He remained off the American coast only between the 10th and the 16th because his fuel supply was running low. His cruise took 248,000 litres of oil in addition to what he had to get from *U140* off the Faeroes.

Sims had cabled Naval Operations in Washington on August 7 that "we feel so certain that minelaying submarine will operate in Vineyard Sound and Nantucket Sound August 10 that counter measures in mining are recommended."[386] Nothing was done, however, in spite of a legend that the American submarine *E2* was in hot pursuit of the submarine and drove her away from Cape Hatteras. "Later, *U117's* commander recalled: 'There was one little Yankee submarine that pretty nearly got me. He got so near that it wasn't any fun.'"[387] If *E2* ever sighted *U117*, however, it was only when the German vessel was homeward-bound. The war diary of *U117* frequently refers to diving before American planes but does not mention an American submarine.

THE NEW CRUISERS: *U140*

The first of the new cruisers to sail was *U140*, under the command of Kophamel. He had previously commanded the Mediterranean U-boats and then had taken *U151* to the Azores and the African coast. Holder of the order Pour le mérite, he was one of the most experienced captains in the German Navy. In *U140* he was to attack shipping off the Nantucket Light Ship and the entrance to New York harbour until *U117*, expected to operate to the south, began her homeward voyage. He could then attack shipping anywhere between Nantucket and Cape Hatteras.

The new boat had problems. When Kophamel had presided over her trials he found her highly unreliable. Leaks, instability, periscope trouble, engine failures followed almost without interruption. At the end of April 1918 the instability led to extensive rebuilding and the attachment of a 15-ton wooden belt, as in the later *U142*. [388] Two basic difficulties remained when he sailed. The boat was not well built and she was not stable. After this cruise, indeed, U-Boat Command asked the Naval Staff why she had been sent out to cross the Atlantic. Kophamel himself blamed the Germania Yard for the U-boat's woes.

She sailed on July 2 and headed up into the North Sea, there to be slowed by strong winds and heavy seas. Kophamel noted that "the stability of the boat is very poor." He gave no details in his war diary,[389] but a German naval architect of the time knew of "larger submarines" that "often, in submerging, took a list to port or starboard of as much as fifty-five degrees." Birch notes that "during her voyage across the Atlantic, *U140* complained that in a high wind the boat took on a list of 35 degrees and remained in that position as the water would not run off the superstructure."[390] The British were soon aware of the problem. A prisoner taken off *UB110* reported on the "unsatisfactory submerged stability and the difficulty experienced in maintaining a trim" on both *U139* and *U140*.

On July 15 Nauen ordered Kophamel to report his position. He gave it and related how that morning he had sighted four huge liners about fourteen miles away, on a 50-degree course toward France at twenty knots. They were *Mauretania* and the ex-German *George Washington*, *Kronprinzessin Cecelie*, and *Kaiser Wilhelm II*, all in service as troop transports. Half an hour later they were out of sight. His signal was not received at home, and in his later report he referred to "the completely inadequate condition" of his radio. Cruiser Command commented critically that this had been "the most valuable of all enemy convoys."

On July 26 and 27 *U140* unsuccessfully attacked shipping off the coast. She attacked *British Major* twice, firing 130 shells the first time, seventy-one the second. Allo signals showed Kophamel that *U156* must be about two hundred miles to the west, but he maintained radio silence. On the 29th a signal from the steamer *Osterley*, about sixty miles away, revealed the presence of *U156* again: "3859-6809 *Osterley* chased." This time Kophamel imitated American calls in order to ask *Osterley* her course and speed but got no answer. That day he chased the British steamer *Vitrubia* without success, and east of Delaware Bay the next day he fired a torpedo at the American *Kermanshah* but missed. Later he tried to make contact with *U156* but without result. On August 1, however, he successfully torpedoed the Japanese *Tokuyama Maru* (7029 tons), two hundred miles southeast of New York.

On August 4 *U140* was not far northeast of Cape Hatteras when she encountered the empty Standard Oil tanker *O. B. Jennings* and fired a torpedo that missed. Half an hour later she surfaced and then fired eighty-six shells at the tanker, registering hits in the engine room and the magazine. *Jennings* returned fire but inaccurately. After the crew took to the boats the second officer of the submarine interrogated them, and René Bastin, second officer of the *Jennings*, "urgently requested" to be taken prisoner. Once aboard *U140* he offered information about shipping and shipping routes, though after the war he claimed that his stay was "enforced."[391] On October 18 the U.S. Force Commander wrote to the Secretary of the Admiralty that "considerable suspicion seems to have attached to him on account of certain actions he took in delaying the ship's departure from Plymouth." It had proved impossible to get any information about him.[392]

All in all, Kophamel was well pleased with this sinking. He said to the first mate in a boat, "I got you at last. I knew I would. What damage did the shell in the engine room do?"[393] The next day he was able to sink a 1060-ton schooner; and on the afternoon of August 6 he came four miles west of the Diamond Shoals Lightship (Cape Hatteras) to shell and sink the American steamer *Merak* (3024 tons). According to his artillery record he fired 148 rounds at the steamer. This was not quite the case. Thirty shells were fired at *Merak* before she ran aground and her crew took to the boats. The others were used to sink the lightship itself (590 tons) and attack the British steamer *Bencleuch*. Kophamel claimed that the lightship was making signals to *Merak*, as was indeed the case because she was trying to keep the steamer away from the shoals. *U140* remained nearby for a day, then headed eastward and to the north.

At dawn on August 10, a hundred miles east of Cape Charles, the lookout of *U140* saw a large steamer in the dim light. This was the Brazilian (formerly Woermann Line) *Uberaba*, with a hundred American troops aboard. A shot across her bow brought a signal from the steamer: "Who is which me attacks, give your name please." *U140* ordered her to stop and send a boat, whereupon *Uberaba* turned away and increased speed, sending out calls for help. The submarine followed, firing forty-seven rounds to stop her. Soon after 0900 the call was picked up by an American destroyer, the new *Stringham* under Cdr. Neil E. Nichols, which had left Norfolk the afternoon before on her way to a convoy rendezvous off Bermuda. Twenty minutes after getting the message she sighted the steamer, and after another fifteen minutes the fore top lookout could spot the submarine, which was trying to close the target. After ten minutes she evidently sighted *Stringham* and abruptly dived, leaving a conspicuous oil slick on the surface. The destroyer zigzagged over the slick and proceeded to drop seventeen depth charges, some in a spiral pattern, in about half an hour. A patch of oil five hundred yards long and three hundred yards wide was the result. Shortly after 1100 she continued on her way.

The first of the charges had exploded close to the submarine, and Kophamel had taken her down to 245 feet. Almost at once water began pouring in through a hatch which could not be tightened from inside and from other leaks as well. The bilges could not be pumped out because the destroyer was overhead. Between forty and forty-five tons of water got into the boat, making it hard to steer and maintain trim. Bastin says she took a 40-degree list. To reduce the water pressure she then came up to 130 feet, but many small leaks developed in all the compartments. Kophamel angrily noted that they were due to the incompetence of the Germania Yard which he had noted even before sailing.

When *U140* surfaced at 1400 she found nothing in sight. In his war diary Kophamel criticized the inexperience of the destroyer captain, to which the submarine owed her escape. He should have remained on the spot to sink the U-boat, which was bound to emerge. This may be so, but at least he drove *U140* away from the transport *Uberaba* and, indeed, from the American coast. The U-boat was not leaking before the depth charge attack.

Bastin exaggerated the danger to himself when he claimed that "the aft deck was smashed, and one of the 6-inch guns had disappeared altogether; the wireless was completely gone and the fat part of the conning tower bent to pieces." One might suppose that a photo of "*U140*" printed by Beckmann of *U117* confirmed Bastin's fantasy, but it really shows *U151* after the British destroyer *Parthian* accidentally ran over her in October 1917, producing superficial damage.[394] Stories told by the crew about a mortally damaged destroyer that tried to ram them reflect the same episode, mixed with another legend about *U151*.

This story about *U151* too was greatly exaggerated. Martin Niemöller, "Number one" aboard that U-boat, wrote that the destroyer "must have scraped over us and torn her bottom off and, when sinking, her boilers must have exploded, so that no sign of her remains visible."[395] This too was fantasy, for in fact *Parthian* was damaged only slightly. The emotional narrative presented by Bastin is equally unreliable. He even claimed that the leaking *U140* went down to 415 feet.

Kophamel noticed a large number of small leaks in all compartments, and the next day test dives showed that the leaks increased at thirty meters and that both periscopes were unusable. By the 13th plugs allowed diving to fifteen meters, but after further unsuccessful attacks on shipping Kophamel decided that since he could not stay under water he would return to Germany. The return voyage began on the 21st. *U140* never came close to the American coast after being attacked.

After August 24 *U140* was moving east and north, listening to *U117* on September 5 and *U156* the next day. On the 6th and the 8th she tried to make contact with Rugia but without result. When *U117* heard her she asked the big sister to come to her aid as her oil was running low. She hoped for twenty cubic meters, but *U140* thought she could spare only half that. On the 9th the two U-boats met to plan for the fuel transfer, which took place off the Faeroes three days later. *U140* rigged lines with cartridge boxes across the distance of one to two hundred meters, and in two days it proved possible to transfer twenty-six cubic meters of oil. They had not been needed since her cruise was so brief.[396]

On September 14 the two boats headed east together and on the 17th south through the lines of mines. The next day, south of the barrage, Kophamel was finally able to inform Rugia that he had sunk 30,000 tons of shipping but had broken off his cruise because of oil and water leakage. He reached Kiel on the afternoon of September 20 after a cruise of less than twelve weeks. The Kaiser had already learned that a new submarine cruiser had sunk 30,000 tons. His comment was surely correct. "Not a very good announcement. Unless one of these U-boat cruisers returns home having sunk 100,000 tons the U-boat war serves no purpose."[397]

U139 TO THE AZORES

U139 was the second new submarine cruiser sent to American waters, though Cruiser Command noted that she was still unsatisfactory when she sailed, four months after commissioning. Her commander, von Arnauld, criticized the whole class of boats. "In a surface fight they could hold their own with anything short of really big guns, but submerged it was difficult to manoeuvre for a torpedo shot. They were clumsy and did not swing around quickly, as is necessary for a craft that aims its shot by aiming itself."[398] The British had already learned of these defects from agents and prisoners. In addition, Launburg of *UB52*, captured in May 1918, told them that Arnauld had left the Mediterranean around the end of February in order to commission one of the newer cruisers for service off the American coast. He had commanded *U35* with phenomenal success since November 1915, specializing in the use of gunfire and sinking more tonnage than any other commander. Like Kophamel of *U140* he held the order Pour le mérite. His orders, dated August 16, took him just north of the Azores to the vicinity of Cape Hatteras, then north along the American coast to Halifax and back, but he did not reach American waters.

On his way out he met *U156* off Rockall to give advice about crossing the Northern Barrage and then continued south in stormy weather. Before dawn on October 1 he gave his position as 4634 North, 1108 West, west of the Bay of Biscay. Evidently he had not yet sighted the ships that were to bring him a modest victory but near disaster as well.[399] They appeared later in the morning: a thirty-ship convoy bound from Gibraltar to England and escorted by an armed boarding steamer of 2502 tons, the *Perth* with three 4.7-inch guns. When *U139* appeared, the escort did her best to provide defence. At 1320 the convoy was zigzagging when she exchanged fire with the submarine at ranges from 8800 to 4800 yards. During the brief encounter one shell hit *Perth* and killed a sub-lieutenant. The submarine then dived while the escort hastened to rejoin the convoy. At 1600 the U-boat emerged again and tried to summon other submarines by radio. For another ten minutes *Perth* fired at her, but she was keeping out of range. About an hour later another brief exchange took place, this time between 9500 and 5800 yards. A British paymaster was killed and the U-boat disappeared.

Perth's captain, Cdr. G. L. Parnell, described his opponent in some detail.

> Cruiser bow. Foreside of conning tower quite straight and practically vertical. Conning tower about as high as long. Conspicuous 5-foot range finder on conning tower. Probably trimmed by stern when chasing, but came up until upper deck was practically level for gun action. Not quite so much freeboard as converted mercantile type. Upper deck built up before and abaft conning tower. Guns about midway between conning tower and breakwater, both 5.9. No sign of other guns. Shooting remarkably good. Range 11,000--4,800 yards. Probably did not do more than 9 knots during action.[400]

Perth next had to head for two steamers in distress, *Bylands* (3309 tons) and *Manin* (2691 tons), both laggards from the convoy. The submarine shelled *Bylands* and she went down at once, while Perth picked up her crew soon afterwards and lowered her whaler to examine *Manin*, whose crew had abandoned ship after a shell hit. At this point two patrol boats, *P67* and *P69*, arrived from another convoy sixty miles away while *Perth* left the scene to rejoin the convoy, stopping only to put a patch over a shell hole forward.[401] P67 was picking up *Manin's* crew when a torpedo from *U139* passed ahead of her and hit *Manin* herself.

Pistor, the first gunnery officer of the submarine, reports most fully what happened then.[402] He and two others were with Arnauld in the conning tower and the captain let him look through the periscope just before firing. *Pistor* said, "Damn close." The captain replied, "So what? Fire. Take her down to fifty meters." He wanted to dive under the sinking *Manin*, which then hit the conning tower, denting it and knocking the hatch open. *Pistor* managed to get the hatch shut and locked, but water still came in because of sprung rivets. Finally Arnauld ordered air to all tanks, and the chief engineer also set the bilge pumps going. Later the commander ordered the bilge pumps run so that the boat could be held at a depth of one meter under the surface -- "a strange feeling, since we were blind and the sea was crowded with vessels." The patrols had dropped eight depth charges over the submarine without effect.

According to Arnauld he found a small steamer the very next day with just the cargo he needed. "With the wine we refreshed our bedraggled spirits and with the cement we repaired the conning tower."[403] By the 4th he had repaired the antennae and could make a long range signal. "Started return journey October 1. All periscopes unusable through striking sinking steamer at night. Slight leaks in conning tower, can dive to a shallow depth. Only able to transmit within limits. Have sunk 7000 [tons]."

> The Northern Patrol thereupon waited for the submarine, expected to round Muckle Flugga between midnight of the 9th-10th [October] and midnight 11th-12th. She carries two 5.9" guns, her periscopes are probably damaged, and she can only dive to a small depth.

The orders stated that it was "particularly important" to intercept and destroy this U-boat, but the patrol operation had to be cancelled on the 11th after another signal, made on the 9th, showed that *U139* was continuing on cruise near the Azores.[404] "Am in square 2776 Rupert. Have continued undertaking. Shall operate of necessity on the surface Azores. Radio gear working."

As *U139* headed toward the Azores she sank a Portuguese patrol boat escorting a steamer, but the steamer itself escaped. According to Arnauld's later story she was carrying several homeward-bound American generals. After trying without success to radio *U157* and get news about traffic routes off the Azores, he decided he could still head westward toward American waters. By the morning of the 21st he had reached longitude 30 West and unsuccessfully attacked the American steamer *Muskegee*. That day or the next, however, he received orders to abandon the war against shipping and return to Germany.

The homeward cruise was uneventful. Signals from Germany described the deteriorating military situation, and *U139* replied with position reports. When she put in to Sassnitz in the Baltic with *U152* and *U155*, there was an unlikely rumour that the British were about to attack. The French naval historian Laurens, evidently relying on Arnauld's memories or war diary, tells of reactions to the news of the revolt in the Fleet.[405]

> The captain assembled the crew, brought them up to date on the events of which he had learned in enciphered signals, and asked for loyalty to their commander and the side of order. The crew asked for an hour to consider, then informed him that they could not remain separated from the sailors in revolt. Von Arnauld brought his submarine to Kiel and while his second moored the boat he put on civilian clothing and disembarked.

This last and only cruise of *U139* -- before she served in the French Navy as Halbronn until 1935 -- lasted 64 days but resulted in the sinking of only 6233 tons of shipping, plus 485 tons for the Portuguese patrol. Her success was even slighter than that of *U140*, since she did not reach American waters. The technical defects of both submarines were primarily responsible for their poor performances. In the future, of course, such large submarines would come into their own.

10. INFORMATION AND ACTION

The incessant work of divers and cryptographers made it possible for the British to read most of the signals transmitted by the U-boats, but for the most part the information acquired was undramatically used for routine purposes. It is hard to pinpoint individual U-boats that were damaged or sunk simply because a cipher was broken or a particular message read. We have seen that when boats operated at great distances from their bases, however, and the command tried to control their movements, action could be based on interception, though chance remained a significant factor. Several further stories illustrate the interplay of information with action.

THE FATE OF *UC30*

Encounters with U-boats close to the British Isles show how difficult it was to trace their courses, much less anticipate them. The arduous last homeward voyage of *UC30* provides an example. This submarine passed through the Straits of Dover at the beginning of April, 1917, and on the 4th, when she sank a sailing vessel and the steamer *Hunstanton*, lifeboats from the steamer could see flames emerging from the top of her conning tower. That evening she reported her troubles to her base. She had passed the Straits without incident but now, with one engine out of service and the other with cylinder damage, could make only three knots and would have to return to the north of the British Isles.

Admiral Bayly at Queenstown was informed at once. "An enemy submarine ... about 70 miles southwest of Lands End, apparently with partially disabled engines. Will probably return northabout." Her speed was known, and it was surmised that she could not dive. The Admiralty ordered Bayly to "send any destroyers available."

Nine days later the outward-bound U50 was near St. Kilda when she sighted a distant U-boat and, after receiving the correct response to a recognition signal, made radio contact with UC30 to ask for provisions. The minelayer reported that she had one disabled oil engine that could not be repaired at sea, and could make only three knots. The commander was sure, however, that he could reach home with his twenty-day supply of oil for fuel and lubrication. He sent a boat over with the provisions and asked U50 to radio that he had not laid his mines. That evening she made this signal, and ten destroyers from the Grand Fleet immediately went hunting for the damaged submarine in spite of a gale from the north. On the 14th she was sighted to the northeast off North Rona but to the surprise of her hunters escaped by diving, and three days later she got away from pursuers south of Sumburgh Head (Shetland) by diving again.[406] On the 18th she tried to make radio contact with her base but merely attracted British attention once more, though the hunt for her was not successful.

By the morning of April 19 she had reached a position seventy-five miles west-southwest of Lindesnes and signalled that she had laid no mines but had sunk a 3000-ton steamer and a 400-ton sail on April 4. The next morning she was ordered to report her position again, but there was no reply. The order was repeated on the 21st as a three-day search began with submarines and Zeppelins, but no answer came to any of the calls. She had obviously been sunk. Two weeks later a crewman's corpse came ashore on the Danish coast north of Esbjerg (east of Horns Reef), and still later another near Sundvik.[407]

British forces had already blocked the Blue Route off Horns Reef with 235 mines, found just on the 19th but not swept until the 23rd because of heavy seas. Meanwhile more mines were being laid in quantity, 1308 southwest of the route on the 20th, another 235 north of it on the 22nd. Presumably UC30 ran on to one of the fields.[407] Tebenjohanns, captured from UC44 four months later, knew that she had hit a mine "a few miles from home port." The older British mines were finally achieving results -- or else, as Ruge indicates, these may have been improved mines used in the Bight in the spring of 1917.[408]

Since the British knew UC30 had suffered from engine trouble, they were much interested when a prisoner taken off UC29 (sunk June 7) revealed that the cylinders of this class of U-boat were carefully checked when "a submarine recently failed to return after all of her 12 cylinders had failed." Later they listened with interest to the signals of a sister vessel, *UC31*, which on November 3 reported turning back because the port engine was out of order with a broken thrust-bearing; she was carrying "4-day mines" and had to return rapidly. Again, she reported on December 30 that "one starboard cylinder is scored, starboard engine out of action as now a second cylinder has failed." She survived the mishaps, however.

The engine problems, as well as the mining difficulties of five more minelayers, occurred in submarines built by Vulkan at Hamburg, all belonging to the First Flotilla stationed at Heligoland.[409] Could sabotage have played a part?

THE SINKING OF *U44*

Radio interception played an important part in the sinking of *U44*, homeward after finding few targets off the west coast of Ireland in late July. After informing *U94* on August 1 that he had met nothing but decoy vessels and destroyers, Wagenführ encountered one more decoy, *Chagford*, on the 7th and inflicted so much damage that she later sank. *U44* herself was hit, however, and told *U84*, met the next day, that she was unable to dive.

Late on the evening of August 11 the British destroyer *Oracle*, on patrol off the Norwegian coast, heard radio signals as Wagenführ tried to make contact with his base. At 0200 on the 12th he made the contact and announced his position off Utsire Island, course (SE) to Hantsholm, and estimated time of arrival at Lyngvig Light (south from Hantsholm) early on the 13th. *Oracle* headed south to intercept him, and at 0600 on the 12th sighted a strange ship on the horizon. Two minutes later, evidently spotting the destroyer, the ship hoisted a sail. After three minutes more, a submarine's bow and stern could be made out on either side of the sail, seven miles away. In turn the U-boat spotted *Oracle* and dived but came to the surface six minutes later, then dived once more. This time after only two minutes the bow appeared again, then the stern as the submarine crash dived. Though *Oracle's* guns missed, the destroyer struck the U-boat's hull at 27 knots and cut through between the top of the conning tower and the stern, still four feet above water, dropping a depth charge as she went over. The submarine's bow came up for a moment; then there was nothing but wreckage from the hull lining and a vast quantity of oil. The destroyer's bow was smashed but she got home. German ships and aircraft looked for *U44* for the next two days, while the British read their signals with interest.

Intelligence studies of U-boat signals wrongly suggested that Wagenführ had been the captain who torpedoed the steamer *Belgian Prince* west of Ireland on July 31, ordered survivors on to the U-boat's deck, smashed the boats and removed lifebelts, took the master below, and then submerged. Three who had kept their belts were picked up eleven hours later. By August 6 the Admiralty had prepared an extensive report on the episode[410] and soon used it in the interrogation of Tebenjohanns of *UC44*. "I cannot explain the incident in any way," said this captain, "except that there are bound to be a few black sheep in any large community; I cannot, however, conceive that any of the submarine commanders whom I know would commit such an atrocity." In December survivors from *U48* named *U44* as the submarine involved, "subsequently lost about August last," though they described Wagenführ as a "good-natured man and capable submarine officer."

In fact it was not Wagenführ who sank Belgian Prince, but Werner of *U55*. Werner's war diary merely records the torpedoing of an unidentified steamer in a heavy sea, but a post-war letter that refers to the true account is appended to it. Spindler corrected the diary entry without giving any details.[411]

NEWS OF U-BOATS TO THE ADRIATIC

At the end of 1917 three new UB-boats were sent to reinforce the Adriatic flotillas. *UB66* reached Cattaro December 9 but survived little more than a month. *UB68* signalled from the Baltic on the 15th and west of southern Ireland on the 23rd; presumably she was heading for Cattaro, where she arrived safely. *UB69* made a signal off Borkum on December 26, then two more as she moved westward through the English Channel. She was sunk while attacking a convoy off Bizerta on January 8. In these instances the interception of signals seems to have served only to track the courses of the submarines and did not lead to sinkings.

The situation was somewhat different for three more UB-boats sent out soon after their trials in the spring of 1918. *UB70* had sailed in February and arrived west of the Orkneys before signalling that she had to return because of damage to her diving rudders. Only in April were she and her sisters *UB71* and *UB105* ready to sail. By this time the Admiralty were well aware of their intentions because of radio intercepts as well as reports from agents in Rome and elsewhere.

On April 4 *UB71* left Kiel with *UB105*, but the next evening *UB105*, proceeding in Danish waters in the Little Belt, was lightly rammed astern by *UB71* and, half an hour later, ran aground. Soon after midnight she radioed for help but heard no response. After stranding for twenty-five hours she returned to Kiel for repairs and refuelling. Her misadventure received a good deal of attention. An item about the stranding of "*U105*" appeared in the *New York Times* three days later, and a photograph, valuable as a study of the UB-III class, soon came into Allied hands. The ONI copy of the photo is dated April 12, though there is also a May 16 date and the note "Received from French General Staff."[412]

On April 13 Nauen radioed *UB71* that *UB105* had finally sailed again on the 11th. On the 16th an intercepted signal from *UB71* located her three hundred and fifty miles west of Ushant and indicated no difficulties thus far. Both submarines were informed the next day that *UB70* had also sailed. Signals from and to Nauen thus made it quite clear to all listeners that the U-boats' destination was the Mediterranean.

The signal from *UB71* also gave a definite basis for estimating the time of her arrival at Gibraltar. Newbolt summarizes thus:[413]

> On April 17 Admiral Heathcoat Grant ordered such vessels as he could assemble for the purpose to occupy successive patrol lines near the Straits of Gibraltar, and four days later *UB71* was sunk by motor launch No. 413 ... whilst on her way to Pola to reinforce the Adriatic Flotilla.

In fact, she was nearly through the Straits, speeding eastward on the surface, when she encountered the patrols near Ceuta. *ML413* heard her engines, saw a large bow wave, and switched on her bow lights to avoid collision. The U-boat abruptly changed course, passed about thirty feet ahead, and dived. Four depth charges followed her down. No further sound was heard, and the wooden wreckage found at daybreak included "parts of a mahogany door pitted with metal fragments."

The success was obvious, but Hall was alarmed at the danger of unveiling the secret about interception. The sailing orders issued the patrols by the Chief of Staff Gibraltar had stated that "three enemy submarines are expected to attempt passage of the Straits from west to east in the course of the next few days." On May 6 Hall criticized this aspect of the orders. [414]

> I would call attention to paragraph 1 of Sailing Orders No. 353 of the 17th April attached. The information in this paragraph is obtained from Nav[al] Intell[igence] telegrams. There has been no attempt at camouflaging the information to make it appear that it had been obtained from sinkings or sightings; the circulation of the Sailing Orders is necessarily large, and the result has been that one of our lines of intelligence is seriously imperilled. If the officer who drew up the sailing orders had appreciated the value the Admiralty attach to the source of these Navintell telegrams, he would certainly have put the information in a different form.

At the end of April *UB70* and *UB105* were still on passage. Nauen informed the three boats on the 29th that at Gibraltar the patrols were very strong and that they should watch out for motor boats. That day *UB70* was west of Gibraltar, where she sank the collier *Valdivia*. On May 5 she signalled that she had passed the Straits on the Spanish side and was heading for Cattaro, but nothing more was heard from her. The wartime guess that she was depth charged on May 8 is mistaken, since the submarine under attack was *U38*. The cause of her disappearance is unknown.

UB105 made a signal from the Mediterranean on May 1 to give her position and the news of sinking 18,000 tons of shipping. Marschall brought her into Cattaro a week later, the only one of the three to arrive, and was soon awarded the order Pour le Mérite. The Kaiser took a personal interest in the Mediterranean Flotilla and visited it at Pola on November 12, 1917.[415] Now on May 31 he lamented the loss of "a complete flotilla of four submarines," obviously referring to *UB66*, *UB69*, *UB70*, and *UB71*.[416] Only *UB68* under Dönitz and *UB105* under Marschall survived.

LATE EPISODES TO THE NORTH

Four more episodes, reconstructed from American, British, and German records of intercepts, encounters, and searches, tell the stories of how U-boats perished or may have perished.

THE WRECK OF *UB82*

"Grid-Tech-Diver" has definitely discovered the wreck of *UB82*, shelled and depth-charged off Ailsa Craig in the North Channel of the Irish Sea on April 17. It lies at 95 meters and has suffered severe damage on the conning tower and foredeck. "All the hatches are closed, so that obviously none of the complement survived the sinking."[417] The wreckage found on the surface fits this conclusion: It consisted of "fragments of woodwork with brass fittings, a white wooden boat, bits of furniture and living-spaces, a shothole plug, two gratings painted black, a mattress and bedcover, two seamen's caps with ribbons of IV (Rommel) and V (Scharnewski) Untersee Boot Flotille."[418]

THE LOSS OF THE NEW *UB119*

One tale of interception has to do with the new *UB119*, which sailed from Heligoland on April 27, 1918, but did not return. Keyes mistakenly claimed she was sunk in the Straits of Dover on May 11,[419] and I myself twice missed the true explanation of her loss,[420] which was suggested by Dewar in *Submarine Losses Return*. To determine the real cause we must examine her orders and signals. O/L Kolbe, commander of *UB119*,[421] received orders dated April 24 sending her to the northern North Sea and if possible to the waters north of Ireland. If she should go as far as the North Channel she was to report from west of Scotland, since her crew lacked training.[422] Three signals made on April 30 located her WSW of Lindesnes, Norway. "No further news," says Spindler.[423] A signal intercepted by the British, however, shows that she spent two days east of Aberdeen and Peterhead and, after reporting from near Fair Isle on May 2 at 1042, was pursued for four hours by trawlers with hydrophones. At the same time on the morning of the 3rd another signal placed her near North Rona. At 0300 on the 4th she gave her position west of the Hebrides, off Flannan Island, and reported that earlier she had not encountered traffic off Aberdeen or Peterhead. Eight hours later she was west of South Uist, obviously heading south.

According to her commander's usual procedure, he should have made another signal about an hour before noon on May 5, but no further signals were picked up. An encounter around that time may have led to the destruction of the U-boat. The steamer *Green Island*, steering WNW between Rathlin Island and the Irish coast, sighted a periscope rising about twenty yards ahead and turned to ram it. The periscope dipped, but *Green Island* bumped heavily over an object under water and on turning back found large amounts of oil on the surface.[424] If this was *UB119*, of course, she did not torpedo a steamer off Belfast on May 25.[425] Indeed, her radio silence after earlier regular signals suggests she had been sunk.

It may be that *UB119* was avoiding the centre of the North Channel, where the American minelayer *Baltimore* had laid four deep lines of mines, three of which blew up just on May 5 after one mine detonated in an experimental skimming sweep.[426] They had been laid across the route *UB119* must have followed. Cowie writes that there was "a marked reduction of U-boat activity in the area," either because of the mine explosions or, more probably, because of "improved anti-submarine measures then coming into play."[427] Ramming by *Green Island* was effective, if not "improved."

THE SINKING OF *UB65*

Evidence for this case consists only of the report from Lt. P. F. Foster, commander of *AL2*, on July 10, 1918, about a German submarine.

On July 10 "at 1825...the U.S. submarine *AL2* sighted something resembling a buoy 3 miles distant on starboard bow, and altered course to investigate. At 1830 a severe explosion shook the boat, putting out lights, &c., and at the same time a large column of water was thrown into the air 80 yards on her starboard quarter. Immediately after this subsided, about six feet of a periscope was seen in the disturbed water. *AL2* dived and helm was put hard astarboard in the hope of ramming. S/m passed very close to the enemy, whose propellers could be distinctly heard through the hull. Listening on C Tube it was ascertained that there were two S/m's in the vicinity, one ahead and the other nearly astern. The engines of the one to the northward, whose periscope had been sighted after the explosion, could be heard running at high speed, another one to the southward was running at moderate speed. *AL2* turned to keep in touch with the S/m to the northward, but at 1855 all sounds from this one ceased, and after circling in the vicinity for two hours *AL2* resumed course for Bantry Bay."[428] The U-boat repeatedly signalled dash-dash-dash-dot or "OE."[429]

A letter dated 7 January 1919 in the National Archives[430] says that "with reference to Admiralty letter of the 17 August last relative to an attack on the 10th July 1918 by U. S. Submarine *AL2*, according to later information it can be definitely stated that the submarine "RVO" did not return to her base, and it is considered that the explosion witnessed by *AL2* resulted in the destruction of the submarine." (RVO or THO was the call sign of *UB65*.) If RVO was really making signals (not noted in German records) to another German submarine (not recorded by any U-boat), the survivor must have been sunk before returning home. Notices of the cruise of *UB65* (II Flotilla) from Helgoland to the Bristol Channel had begun with three torpedoes fired by *D6* at 0310 on July 4 in 5658/0419E, as reported by THO.

THE LAST CRUISE OF *UB90*

The last cruise of *UB90* shows what could be gleaned from interception. Because of the danger from mines along the swept channels in the Bight of Heligoland, von Mayer sailed from Kiel on September 23 and took the route through the Kattegat and Skagerrak. Four days later a signal showed that he was off Peterhead, and the Northern Patrol supposed that he then passed Fair Isle on her way north. In fact, as a signal made on the homeward voyage revealed, *UB90* went through the Pentland Firth. Most of the time she could remain on the surface, though she had to dive to forty meters to avoid a patrolling motorboat.

Around noon on October 3 she reached the waters west of Loop Head, Ireland, at the mouth of the Shannon. The British tanker *Eupion* (3575 tons), out from Norfolk, Virginia, had almost arrived at Foynes, County Limerick, when a Spanish lookout in her crow's nest reported something ahead. His lack of English meant that no one could be sure what he said, but the master steered for the object. Ten minutes later the lookout reported running over the top of it; indeed, an American naval signalman on board stated later that this lookout had sighted a U-boat's periscope and conning tower four times. At about 1530, now just ten miles west of Loop Head, the submerged U-boat fired a torpedo at five hundred yards range, blowing a large hole in the tanker's hull and perhaps detonating a boiler. The boat then came to the surface and circled the sinking steamer, while crewmembers took photographs and waved off the ship's lifeboat and raft. Reports differed as to what the Germans shouted. Was it "Keep clear of sinking ship" or "Get to hell out of it"? More to the point, both the naval signalman and the chief officer described the submarine as equipped with jumping wires, with insulators, only between the bow and the conning tower. Presumably the jumping wires aft had been torn free when *Eupion* ran over the submarine.

Very early on the morning of October 5 *UB90* made a signal to her base in cipher Gamma Alpha which the British could not read, doubtless trying to report the difficulties due to her encounter with *Eupion*. (The message was not received at home, perhaps because of antenna difficulties.) She then gradually made her way up the Irish coast and on the 11th arrived in Vaag Fiord on Syderoe in the Faröe Islands, where she got rid of the wire wrapped around her propellers. News of her visit reached the Northern Patrol three days later, after the British consul at Vaag reported that "a large German submarine with one gun had anchored outside the bay with a wire around her propellers, this she cleared and sailed at 2000."[431] News of the event came too late to be useful, but the return of the submarine to her base could be anticipated.

As early as the evening of the 12th *UB90* was north of the Shetlands reporting her misadventure. Only the British received most of her signal and could piece together the story. She had sunk 3575 tons in October but had fouled her propellers and diving rudder. After repairs off the Faeroes she could now make seven knots on the surface and was on her way home via Peterhead. A continuation of the signal stated that Pentland Firth was viable. Evidently this part of the signal was also received at home, for on October 18 U-boats were told that the route was open. The next day she repeated her signals, and on the 14th, steadily moving eastward, she asked to be picked up by minesweepers on the 18th. She described her routes in the Pentland Firth and, more recently, through Area A of the Northern Barrage. She was still transmitting with difficulty, for large sections of these signals were not received at home. The British now knew she had sunk the 3575-ton *Eupion* and that wires had then fouled propellers and diving rudder. Her speed was still reduced and therefore she might be intercepted.

When the British submarine *L12* sailed on the 11th to patrol near Skagen she received no special orders about the U-boat, then still in the Faeroes. Within the next few days as signals came in, however, she must have been warned to intensify her watch. In any event, on the afternoon of the 16th she "sighted enemy submarine 30 degrees on starboard bow" and proceeded to attack submerged. Twenty minutes later she was in a position to fire four bow torpedoes. Surfacing after the explosion, she found nothing but a pool of oil four hundred yards in diameter and what looked like half a corpse. Two days later the British intercepted a German message: "*UB90* did not arrive tonight." The next day came a question: "Has *UB90* been picked up?" The answer was negative.

REVISED LIST OF GERMAN SUBMARINES SUNK OR INTERNED

Locations are N and E unless otherwise stated. Forces are British unless otherwise stated (Am = American, Fr = French, Ger = German, Russ = Russian). Other abbreviations are C = Convoy, Cr = Cruiser, D = Destroyer, D/c = Depth-charge, G = Gunfire, Int = Interned, M = Mine, P = Patrol, Q = Decoy, R = Ram, Slp = Sloop, S/m = Submarine, Stm = Steamer, Str = Stranded, Sw = Sweep. Special signs are these: * = Wartime divers to wreck, (*) but not identified; ** = Also salved, # Identified by modern divers.

The list is corrected from my earlier version in *U-Boat Intelligence*, 182-190, largely by use of Messimer, *Verschollen*; Termote, *Verwenden in de Noordzee*; McCartney, *Lost Patrols*; and http//uboat.net/fates/ losses.html; along with valuable information from Kendal McDonald and Innes McCartney.

Date	No.	Lat/Long	Area	Explanation
			1914	
Aug 9	U15	5835/0156	Fair Isle	R Cr *Birmingham*
Aug 12	U13	Unknown	Helg Bight	Unknown
Nov 23	U18	5841/0255W	Scapa Flow	R trawler
Dec 9	U11	5120/0252	Zeebrugge	M #
Dec 18	U5	5129/0311	Zeebrugge	M
			1915	
Jan	U31	Unknown	East Coast	Unknown
Jan 21	U7	5343/0602	Dutch coast	T *U22*
Mar 4	U8	5056.04/0115.38	Folkestone	Sw D *Gurkha* P #Batchelor
Mar 10	U12	5607/0220W	Fife Ness	R trawler P

Mar 18	U29	5816/0059	N Sea N	R *Dreadnought*
Apr 1+	U37?	5049/0045	Dungeness	Unknown (*) 1917 (McCartney writes: # Belgian coast)
May	UB3	Unknown	Aegean Sea	Unknown
Jun 5	U14	5713/0033	Peterhead	G Q trawler
Jun 23	U40	5700/0150W	Aberdeen	T C-24 (+ Q)
Jul 2	UC2	5226/0148	Yarmouth	R + M (own) *
Jul 20	U23	5855/0014	Fair Isle	T C-27 (+ Q)
Jul 24	U36	5907/0530W	Hebrides	G Q *Prince Charles*
Aug 16	UB4	5246/0210	Yarmouth	G trawler
Aug 19	U27	5043/0722	W Scillies	G Q *Baralong*
Aug end	U26	Unknown	Gulf of Finland	M (Rus)
Sep 15	U6	5910/0509	Stavanger	T *E16*
Sep 24	U41	4910/0723	W Scillies	G Q *Baralong*
Oct 21	UC9	5147/0140	Longsand	M (own)
Nov 15	UC8	Terschelling	L. V.	Stranded, int
Nov 29	UC13	4100/3008	Black Sea	Stranded
			1916	
Mar 16	UC12	4030/1715	Taranto	M (own) **
Mar 22	U68	5154/1053W	SW Ireland	G Q *Farnborough*
Apr 5	UB26	4928/0002	Le Havre	Nets, d/c Fr *Trombe* **
Apr 25	UB13	5133/0235	Zeebrugge	M

Apr 27	UC5	5203/0146	Shipwash	Stranded **
May 27	U74	5710/0120	Peterhead	G trawlers P
May 27	UC3	5135/0308	Zeebrugge	M
June	U10	Unknown	Gulf of Finland	M (Russ)
Jul 5	UC7	5122/0307	Zeebrugge	M
Jul 7+	U77	5604/0230W	North Sea N	http.uboat.net/wwi
Jul 14	U51	5355/0753	Ems Estuary	T *H5* P *1968
Aug 4+	UB44	Unknown	Aegean Sea	Unknown
Aug 21	UC10	5145/0320	Schouwen Bank	T *E54* P #
Oct 1	UB7	4430/3400	Sebastopol	Seaplane (Russ) P
Nov 3	U56	Unknown	Lapland	D (Russ)
Nov 4	U20	5633/0908	Jutland	Stranded #1984
Nov 6	UB45	4315/2800	Varna	M (Russ)
Nov 14	UC15	4500/3000	Sulina	M (own or Ger)
Nov 30	UB19	4956/0245W	Channel	G Q *Penshurst*
Dec 6	UC19	4941/0630W	Channel	Sw D *Ariel* P
Dec 7	UB46	4126/2835	Sulina	M (Russ) * #
Dec 13	UB29	5109/0146	SE Goodwins	D/c D *Landrail* P

1917

Jan 14	UB37	5010.20/0138.40W	Channel	G Q *Penshurst* # I. McCartney, 1999
Jan 22	U76	7100/2400	North Cape	G (Russ) + storm

138

Feb 8	UC46	5106.86/0137.15	SE Goodwins	R D *Liberty* P
				# D. Batchelor & R. Peacock
Feb 8	UC39	5356/0006	Flamborough	D/c D *Thrasher* P* '18
Feb 17	U83	5134/1123W	SW Ireland	G Q *Farnborough*
Feb 19	UC18	4915/0234W	Channel	G Q *Lady Olive*
Feb 23	UC32	5454.521/0119.320W		M (own) *
				#Sunderland SAC, 1989
Mar 10	UC43	6057/0111W	Muckle Flugga	T *G13* P
Mar 12	U85	4952/0320W	Start Point	G Q *Privet*
Mar 13	UC68	5017/0331W	Start Point	M (Ger) ?
Mar 13	UB6	Maas	Dutch coast	Stranded, int
Apr 21	UC30	5520/0715	Horns Reef	M
May 1	U81	5133/1338W	NW Ireland	T *E54* P
May 8	UC26	5103/0140	Calais	R D *Milne* P
				# R. Peacock
May 10	UC76	in port	Heligoland	M (own)
May 14	U59	5533/0715	Horns Reef	M (Ger)
May 15?	UB39	5102/0206	Barrage	M #
May 18	UC36	Unknown	Needles	Unknown
May 21	UB36	4842/0514W	Ushant	R steamer C
May 24	UC24	4206/1819	Cattaro	T *Circe* (Fr) P
Jun 7	UC29	5150/1150W	S Ireland	G Q *Pargust*
Jun 12	UC66	4956/0510W	Lizard	D/c trawler P

Jul 7	U99	5800/0300	North Sea	N T *J2* P
Jul 12	U69	6025/0132?	North Sea N?	D/c D *Patriot* P?
Jul 19	UC1	Unknown	Nieuport?	M?
Jul 26	UC61	5054/0139	Gris Nez	Stranded
Jul 28	UB20	5121/0238	Ostend	M#
Jul 29	UB27	5247/0224	Smiths Knoll	D/c gunboat *Halcyon* P
Jul 30	UB23	4957/0515W	Lizard	D/c *P60*, int
Aug 4	UC44	5207/0659W	Waterford	M (own) **
Aug 12	U44	5851/0420	Stavanger	R D *Oracle* P
Aug 20	UC72	4600/0848W	Biscay	G Q *Acton*
Aug 21	UC41	5602/0243W	Dundee	M (own) *
Aug 31	U50	5410/0445	Terschelling	M
Sep 2	U28	7234/2756	North Cape	Explos munitions stm
Sep 3	U66	5410/0445?	Terschelling?	M
Sep 5	U88	5410/0445	Terschelling	M
Sep 10	UC42	5145/0813W	Cork	M (own) *
Sep 11	U49	4617/1442W	W Biscay	R munitions stm
Sep 12	U45	5548/0730W	W Shetlands	T *D7* P
Sep 14?	UC21	Unknown	To Channel	M?
Sep 22	UB32	5145/0205	Sunk LV	Aircraft bomb P?
Sep 26	UC33	5155/0614W	St Georges Ch	R *P61* C

Sep 27	*UC6*	5130/0134	N Foreland	M (*)
Sep 29	*UC55*	6008/0100W	Lerwick	Accident? G D P
Oct 3	*UC14*	5120/0310E	Zeebrugge	M
Oct 4	*UC16*	perhaps off Zeebrugge		M
Oct 5	*UB41*	5418/0021W	Scarborough	M (Ger?)
Oct 7	*U106*	5400/0435?	Texel	M
Oct 14	*UC62*	5030/0220W	Portland	M # (?) Found on Thornton Bank 2002
Nov 1	*UC63*	5123/0200	S Goodwins	T *E52* P
Nov 3	*UC65*	5030.25/0028.37	Dartmouth	T *C15* P #
Nov 17	*UC51*	501152/0417.18W	Start Point	M # I.McCartney
Nov 17	*U58*	5137/0812	Milford Haven	D/c US D *Fanning* C
Nov 18	*UC47*	5403/0022	Flamborough	R *P57* P # S.Carr & C.Davis 1997
Nov 18?	*UC57*	Unknown	Gulf of Finland	M (Russ)
Nov 24	*U48*	5117/0131	SW Goodwins	Stranded + G P (*) Wreck surfaces from time to time
Nov 29	*UB61*	5325/0458	Vlieland	M
Dec 2	*UB81*	5029.22/0058.12W	Owers	M #
Dec 6	*UC69*	4957/0110W	Barfleur	Collision *U96*
Dec 9	*UB18*	4917/0547W	Channel	R trawler C
Dec 10	*UB75*	Unknown	Flamborough	M
Dec 13	*U75*	5357/0537	Terschelling	M

Date	Boat	Position	Location	Notes
Dec 14	UC38	3832/2034	Ionian Sea	D/c FrD escort
Dec 19	UB56	5056.81/0123.10	Dover Barr	M (*) # D.Batchelor
Dec 25	U87	5256/0507W	Irish Sea	D/c R P56 C

1918

Date	Boat	Position	Location	Notes
Dec-Jan	U93	Unknown	W Channel	Unknown (?#5017.9/0321.25W)
Jan 7	U95	4959/0512W	W Channel	R stm
Jan 8?	UC50	5052.80/0057.13	Dungeness	R, D/c Zubian #
Jan 9	UB69	3730/1038	Bizerta	Sw slp Cyclamen C
Jan 14+	UB63	To Channel,	Ire Sea	Unknown
Jan 18	UB66	Unknown	Mediterranean	Unknown
Jan 19	UB22	5427/0635	Helix Bight	M
Jan 26	U109	5053/0131	Dover Barr	G P, M (?)
Jan 26	U84	5153/0544W	St Georges Ch	R P62 P
Jan 26	UB35	5103/0146	East of Calais	D/c D Levin P # T. Termote
Feb 8	UB38	5057.85/0121.63	Dover Barr	M (*) #
Feb 12	U89	5538/0732W	N Channel	R cry Rexburg C
Mar 10	UB58	5100.11/0118.58	Dover Barr	M # D. Batchelor
Mar 15	U110	5549/0806W	N Ireland	D/c D
Mar 15?	UB17	Unknown,	out to W Channel Mar. 11	
Mar 19?	UB54	Unknown	Dover Barr?	M (*)?

Mar 24	UC48	5022/0147W	Wight	D/c D *Loyal* C; int
Mar 26	U61	5148/0552W	Irish Sea	R *PC51* C
Apr 11	UB33	5056.03/0117.98	Dover Barr	M * # D.Batchelor
April	UC79	5055/0134	Gris Nez	M (*?)
				Found off Belgian coast
Apr 17	UB82	5513/0515W	N Channel	D/c drifters P
				# T. Cecil & Grid-Tech-Diver
Apr 19	UB78	5101.03/0116.48E	Dover Barr	M(*) #
Apr 21	UB71	3558/0518W	Gibraltar	D/c *ML413* P
Apr 22	UB55	5101.32/0119.78	Dover Barr	M * #
Apr 25	U104	5159/0626W	St Georges Ch	D/c slp *Jessamine* P
Apr 30	UB85	5447/0527W	Irish Sea	G slp *Coreopsis* P
May 2	UB31	5102.06/0110.22	Dover Barr	D/c dry *Lord*
	Leitrim*#			
May 5	UB119	5516/0624W	Rathlin Is	R stm *Green Island* #?
May 5+	UB70	Unknown	E Gibraltar	Unknown
May 8	U32	3607/1328	Sicilian Sea	D/c slp *Wallflower* C
May 9	UC78	4950/0140W	Channel	R tramps Q *Alexandra*
May 10	UB16	5206/0201	Outer Gab bard	T *E34* P (*)
May 11	U154	3645/1200W	W St Vincent	T *E35* P
May 12	U103	4916/0451W	W Channel	R tramps *Olympic*
May 12	UB72	5006.58/0250.58W	Lyme Bay	T *D4* P
				# I. McCartney
May 17	UC35	3948/0742	Sardinia	G Fr *Ally* P

May 18	U39	3640/0007	Cartage	Bomb Fr planes, int
May 23	UB52	4136/1825	Taranto Barr	T H4 P
May 24	UC56	Channel	Scamander	Mach dam, int
May 26	UB74	5031.48/0233.34W	Lyme Bay	D/c yacht Lorna C*#
May 31	UC75	5356.28/0009.04	Flamborough	R D Fairy C #B. Thompson, 1989
Jun 17	U64	3807/1207	Mediterr	G D Lychnis C
Jun 20	UC64	5058.530/0123.213	Dover Barr	M * # D. Batchelor
Jun 26	UC11	5155/0141	Sunk LV	M (Ger) *
Jul 4?	UB108	?Dover Barr	Unknown	Unknown
Jul 5	UB1	N Adriatic	Caorlé	M**
Jul 10	UB65	(?)5107/0942W	S Ireland	Accident
Jul 12+	UC77	Unknown	Dover Barr?	M?
Jul 19	UB110	5439/0055W	Middlesboro	R, d/c D Garry C**
Jul 20	UB124	5543/0751W	N Ireland	D/c D C
Jul 28+	UB107	5408/0000W	E Coast	Unknown #
Aug 3	UB53	3958/1901	Otranto Barr	M
Aug 8	UC49	5019,9/0330W	Plymouth	D/c D C #
Aug 13	UB30	5432.351/0035.671W	Whitby	D/c trawler C * #G. Fox, July 1993
Aug 14	UB57	5156/0202E	Zeebrugge	M
Aug 15	UB103	5054/0129	Dover Barr	D/c P, M (not found)
Aug 19+	UB12	Unknown	N Downs	Unknown

Aug 28	UC70	5431.599/0040.131W	Whitby	Air bomb, d/c C * #D. Foster, 1992
Aug 29	UB109	5103.73/0114.13	Dover Barr	M (shore) * #
Sep 8	U92	5900/0130W?	N Barr B	M (Am)
Sep 9+	UB127	5915/0130W	N Barr B	M (Am)
Sep 10	UB83	5828/0150W	Pentland	D/c D
Sep 25	U156	5945/0200?	N Barr A	M (Am)
Sep 29	UB115	5514.24/0022.41W	Newton-by-Sea	Air, d/c C # R. Young, 1973?
Sep end	U102	5920/0055?	N Barr A	M (Am)
Sep end	UB104	5930/0044?	N Barr A	M (Am)
Sep end	UB113	Unknown	N Sea N	Unknown
Oct 4	UB68	3556/1620	Malta	G str C
Oct 16	UB90	5755/1027	Skaw	T L12 P
Oct 18	UB123	5945/0220?	N Barr A	M (Am) ?
Oct 21?	U34	Unknown	Ionian Sea	D/c P?
Oct 28	U78	5602/0508	Dogger Bank	T G2 P
Oct 28	UB116	585007/030406W	Scapa Flow	M (shore) * # P.L. Smith, 1980

ABBREVIATIONS

BdU Befehlshaber der U-Booten (Chief of U-Boats)
DID Director of the Intelligence Department
DNI Director of Naval Intelligence
K/K Korvetten-Kapitän (Lieutenant Commander)
K/L Kapitän-Leutnant (Lieutenant)
O/L Oberleutant (Lieutenant)
PG British Number for Tambach Document "pinched from Germans"

NOTES

[1] For the capture of these archives see *Guides to the Microfilmed Records of the German Navy, 1850-1945: No. 1. U-Boats and T-Boats 1914-1918*, vii-ix; also Pearson, *Life of Ian Fleming*, 116-17; Rosenberg and Stewart, *Ian Fleming*, 33.

[2] For microfilm numbers see *Guides to the Microfilmed Records of the German Navy*.

[3] *Simsadus:London*, 103-5; tracking chart for September 1-14, 1918, between 104 and 105.

[4] Newbolt, *Naval Operations* 5.viii.

[5] Von Waldeyer-Hartz, *Admiral von Hipper*, 236-38.

[6] Damant was awarded the OBE on June 11, 1919. On his work and Miller's see Davis, *Deep Diving and Submarine Operations*, 242-57.

[7] Ibid. 247.

[8] *Strange Intelligence*, 197-213 and vii.

[9] *Their Secret Purposes*, 37.

[10] He had already printed the true number, *UB110*, in the *Daily Telegraph*, July 30, 1931.

[11] *Their Secret Purposes*, 37-42; or two months, according to the *Daily Telegraph*. (In fact it was the salving that took eleven weeks.) In any case the dates are impossible.

[12] Spindler, "Herr Hektor Bywater," 412-13.

[13] ADM 116/1851.

[14] James's contemporaries called him "Bubbles" because Pears Soap used a painting of him by his grandfather, the famous painter Millais; cf. interview in Millais, *Sir John Everett Millais*, 18-22.

[15] James, *Code Breakers*, xxii.

[16] Note also the thorough study by Robinson, *Zeppelin*.

[17] Andrew, *Secret Service*, 521 n. 116. These are ADM 137/203 (16 Dec. 1914 to 31 Dec. 1915), 451 (1916), 645 (1917), 868 (Jan.-Apr. 1918), 869 (May-Aug. 1918), and 964 (Sept.-Nov. 1918).

[18] James, op. cit., xx.

[19] Tuchman, *Zimmermann Telegram*, 10; Bright, *Telegraphs in War Time*, 861; Corbett, *Naval Operations*, 1.43. Cables in the Straits: Gladisch, *Nordsee*, 7, Karte 1.

[20] Graves, *Thin Red Lines*, 9-10.

[21] Post Office Archives, POST 83/102.

[22] Brown, *Cable and Wireless*, 4, 10.

[23] POST 83/60.

[24] Brown, op. cit., 4.

[25] POST 83/60, 83/62, 83/102/216.

[26] Corbett, *Naval Operations*, 1.129-30.

[27] ADM 137/1611 and 328.

[28] Brown, op.cit., 18-19.

[29] Corbett, op. cit., 1.290, 379-84.

[30] For cables cut off the American coast in 1918 see Chapter 9.

[31] ADM 137/1262.

[32] Valentiner, Terreur des mers, 175-76.

[33] ADM 137/4155.

[34] Signals located her in 5327/0445E (001 epsilon), then in 5251/0355 (014 alpha VI) where she reported "Made the attempt, returning owing to difficulties." Room 40's comment was that she had "apparently been fishing for a cable." See also ADM 137/4689 for August 30, 1917.

[35] ADM 137/3060 (prisoner from *U103*).

[36] Gladisch, op. cit., 7.24-25

[37] ADM 137/1381, 2089.

[38] ADM 137/3913.

[39] PG 77001.

[40] ADM 137/505.

[41] ADM 137/839.

[42] See Gladisch, op. cit., 6 Karte 16. Bold-face indicates quadrants mentioned in the text.

[43] Spindler, Handelskrieg, 4.271.

[44] Ibid. 4.277.

[45] ADM 137/3913.

[46] PG 62019; Gladisch op. cit., 7.23.

[47] ADM 137/645.

[48] Cowie, Mines, 60, though both Gladisch and Ruge give earlier dates. These mines had "Herz horns" (invented in 1868), glass tubes which when broken released electrolyte and completed firing circuits (Hartmann, Weapons that Wait, 275).

[49] ADM 137/1922.

[50] ADM 137/645.

[51] ADM 137/3906.

[52] Gibson and Prendergast, *German Submarine War*, 316; cf. Bywater, *Their Secret Purposes*, 44-48.

[53] Robinson, *Zeppelin*, 214.

[54] ADM 137/3898.

[55] ADM 137/4689.

56 An Admiralty telegram of April 19 had said they were "expected to be ready June but may be later," while a note added, "acoustic mines probably not till later" (ADM 137/868).

[57] Hartmann, op. cit., 276.

[58] Ruge, *Im Kustenvorfeld*, 17.

[59] Keyes, *Naval Memoirs*, 2.350. An Admiralty report states that the "M mines were laid at 0130 on the 8th, while several explosions <were> heard at 1045" (ADM 137/869).

[60] PG 61866.

[61] ADM 116/1646; Gladisch, op.cit., 7.322-23.

[62] About an hour later the inbound *UB116* took Route B in the opposite direction, reaching Zeebrugge at 0600. Her chart shows that this route began in about 5133N/ 0228E (or 040 beta), passed between the West Hinder Bank and Thornton Ridge, and went on toward Zeebrugge at about 100 degrees (PG 61871).

[63] Spindler, *Handelskrieg* 5.414 (see p. V).

[64] ADM 137/1630.

[65] *UB55, UC75, UB109* (Flanders); *UB85* and *U103* (Bight).

[66] Bywater, *Their Secret Purposes*, 44-48.

[67] Moraht, *Werwolf der Meere*, 150.

[68] Fürbringer of *UB110* implies that he first met him in prison on September 23 (*Alarm! Tauchen!!*, 245).

[69] Something like the prisoner's statement was known to Gibson and Prendergast, who state that "in August the Germans ran a leader-cable along the Thornton Ridge to guide their submarines" (*German Submarine War*, 316).

[70] PG 69299.

[71] Roskill, *Hankey: Man of Secrets*, 1.159 n.1.

[72] James, *Code-Breakers*.

[73] Jeschke, *U-Boottaktik*, 12.

[74] Birch, *Contribution*, 1.94.

[75] Ibid. 99.

[76] Wright, *Spycatcher*, 10-13.

[77] James, op. cit., 68; Beesly, *Room 40*, 69-70.

[78] Beesly, op. cit., 262, 254 n. 1.

[79] Grant, *U-Boat Intelligence*, 57.

[80] Robinson, op. cit., 72, 79-80, 277.

[81] *The Man of Room 40*, 190-91; James, op. cit., 121-22.

[82] Robinson, op. cit., 298 and n. 1.

[83] Ibid. 305, 333.

[84] Walle, "*Anwendung der Funktelegraphie,*" 136 and note 96.

[85] Robinson, op. cit., 313-14; cf. 121-28.

[86] Jones, *Wizard War*, 84-214 (Cleves, 93; chart, 203; west of England, 123.).

[87] Hall, "Rough Notes," 10 January 1936, p. 2, Churchill College Cambridge, Archives Centre HALL 2/1; cited by Andrew, *Her Majesty's Secret Service*, 123.

[88] ADM 137/849.

[89] Beesly, op. cit., 266. He had in mind *UC44, UC64*, and *UC70*.

[90] The British noted "enemy submarine returning home damaged" at 2300 on February 20 (ADM 137/645); cf. Spindler, op. cit., 4.49.

[91] At Helgoland, ibid. 4.62. All these boats belonged to the First Flotilla, though *UC68* from Flanders was probably sunk in the same way on March 13 (ibid. 4.151).

[92] These were five UB-boats: *UB33, UB74, UB109, UB110, UB116,* and five UC-boats:*UC5, UC11, UC32, UC44,* and *UC70.*

[93] ADM 137/203; on the sinking see Groos, Nordsee, 2.253-54. Kemp (H. M. Submarine, 45) wrongly ascribes the sinking to destroyers.

[94] Lorey, *Krieg in den türkischen Gewässern*, 1.114; Walle, "*Anwendung der Funktelegraphie,*" 126 n. 50; British efforts to protect "the details of her construction" in Kemp, op. cit., 64-65; on the sinking, Lorey, op. cit., 2.107-8 ("important individual items" recovered).

[95] Lorey, op. cit., 1.188-89; 2.147-48.

[96] Corbett, op. cit., 3.205-6; Grant, *U-Boat Intelligence*, 134-35; orders quoted by Lorey, op. cit., 1.199.

[97] Birch, *Contribution*, 1.535.

[98] http.//www.ukans.edu/..kansite/ww_one/naval/ae2.htm.

[99] A. Sansoni rightly insists that British cryptographers were reading German messages before the *Magdeburg* book was acquired ("First Ultra Secret", 100-1).

[100] Copy 151, ADM 137/4156.

[101] Mäkalä, *Geheimnis*, 78; cf. 119-31.

[102] Beesly, op. cit., 4-6, 22-26.

[103] ADM 137/203.

[104] Basic materials on these topics are reflected in Beesly, James, and Robinson; Kahn, *Codebreakers*, and *Seizing the Enigma*, 15-24; Rowan, *Story of Secret Service*.

[105] Givierge, *Au service*, 204. I am deeply grateful to David Kahn for the loan of microfilms of Bibliothèque Nationale, Département des Manuscrits, Don 18899 (2 vols.), and N.A.F. 24353--24.355 (2 vols.; vol. 1 to October 15, 1916). Copies of HVB are in ADM 137/4388-89.

[106] Givierge, Au service, 204, 210; *Étude historique*, 338.

[107] Beesly, op. cit., 26-27.

[108] Ibid. 3-7 (22-28). Copies of VB are in ADM 137/4374-75.

[109] Givierge, *Étude historique* 1.497.

[110] Robinson, op. cit., 129.

[111] Givierge, *Au service*, 210-11.

[112] Givierge, *Étude historique*, 1.502. Copies of FVB are in ADM 137/4386-87.

[113] Givierge, *Au service*, 211; *Étude historique*, 1.502; Beesly, op. cit., 26.

[114] Givierge, *Étude historique*, 1.504.

[115] Givierge, *Au service*, 211; *Étude historique* 1.650.

[116] Givierge, *Étude historique*, 1.489-90, 504, 576. Copies of Gamma Alpha are in ADM 137/4515, Gamma Gamma in 4517-18, and Gamma Ulli in 4511-14.

[117] Ibid. 574.

[118] Givierge, *Au Service*, 207; cf. James op. cit., 115.

[119] Beesly, op. cit., 145. Robinson, op cit., 189, identifies it as the "latest secret signal book of the German Navy... changed just after Jutland." (Copies of AFB are in ADM 137/ 4377-83.) The War Diary was also found (ADM 137/3964).

[120] Now in ADM 137/4308-10.

[121] R. Higham in Jordan, ed., Naval Warfare, 96.

[122] ADM 137/4689. A note in the Public Record Office catalogue at ADM 137/4178 describes what Hope did. "Captain (later Admiral) Herbert Hope, an officer on the War Staff in the Admiralty in August 1914, was appointed to Room 40 about October 1914 to vet and comment on all German decrypts. He was, in effect, the head of Room 40, although Sir Alfred Ewing, Director of Naval Education, was officially in charge. He began simply by adding notes and explanations to individual decrypts, but by mid-1915 was keeping a daily diary of events. In 1917 he was posted to sea in the Adriatic and succeeded by Commander (later Admiral) William 'Bubbles' James. His diaries were then continued as Room 40's official War Diary."

[123] Givierge, *Au service*, 213; *Étude historique*, 2.374.

[124] Robinson, op. cit., 219.

[125] Givierge, *Étude historique*, 2.243-45.

[126] ADM 137/4249, from *UC44*.

[127] Robinson, op. cit., 230 n.1.

[128] PG 61710.

[129] ADM 137/4689; cf.4171.

[130] ADM 116/1632, 137/4248, 137/4249, 137/4251.

[131] Andrew, *Secret Service*, 123, calls this FFB but this may not be right.

[132] Harbord, *American Army in France 1917-1919*, 157.

[133] Rowan, op. cit., 732 n. 11.

[134] List in ADM 137/3964; *Marineliste und Morsenamen*, ADM 137/4311.

[135] ADM 137/4311-12.

[136] Rowan, op. cit., 662, assigns the chart to *L51*, which was not in the air. Log book of *L45*, ADM 137/3964, which states that the codebooks came from *L44* (probably an error).

[137] Letter of May 15, 1936, in PG 61714.

[138] ADM 116/1634 and 137/2100.

[139] PG 61626. The orders of *U62* instructed her to use a new cipher after June 1,1918.

[140] ADM 137/1459.

[141] Walle, "Anwendung," 118 n.26.

[142] PG 69299.

[143] Not, as in the earlier chart, citing quadrant, Greek letter, and number.

[144] ADM 116/1851.

[145] ADM 137/4377.

[146] ADM 137/4270.

[147] ADM 137/4531 (April 1919); cf. 4519.

[148] ADM 137/645. Identifications from Funknamenliste aboard *UC44*, ADM 137/4251.

[149] ADM 137/645. Confirmations from Funknamenliste of *UC44*, ADM 137/4251, cited above.

[150] The 1919 Memorandum on Call-Signs wrongly suggests that the Germans never used the second column because they thought it had been compromised in a Zeppelin disaster on October 20 (see below).

[151] ADM 137/645.

[152] ADM 137/868. Flotillas are from Funknamenliste Heft 2 (ADM 137/4334).

[153] For one thing, the Fifth Flotilla had been disbanded on May 19.

[154] ADM 137/3875.

[155] ADM 137/869.

[156] ADM 137/869.

[157] ADM 137/964; dates, ADM 137/4519; a copy of the list, ADM 137/4335.

[158] ADM 137/964; cf. 645.

[159] Dorwart, *Office of Naval Intelligence*, 123. For their recruitment and activities cf. Fitzgerald, *The Knox Brothers*, 134-39, 142-45.

[160] Dorwart, op. cit., 106.

[161] James, op. cit., 29; cf. Beesly, op. cit., 14-16.

[162] Beesly, op. cit., 177; Marder, *Dreadnought to Scapa Flow* 4.267-68.

[163] Beesly, op. cit., 261-62.

[164] *Naval Investigation* 1.106-7.

[165] Last page of ADM 137/4689: "for Capt James from G.H.F. 1.X.18 " Tracing of routes on Flanders coast is "hampered by the fact that messages in June and July, when Route 3 was in use, have not yet been decoded, and the August messages only partially so. The following results seem to be well based: B' route was largely used in April and May: what may be called the 'gathering squares' from which the submarines signalled were 907 (old 30) and 858 (old 8). The route is given by a message to WHK and ...runs between Raabs Head and Thornton Ridge on Wenduyne, turning off when the Mole bears about 110 deg. 3' route was more in evidence in June and July; the gathering squares being apparently 808 (old 7) and 859 (old 170). There is reason to believe that leads it about 186 deg., from the point on the

Middel Bank where several tracks are shown to meet, to Z between Schooneveld and Raan Banks. A' route is almost the only route used in September and August: the rendez-vous for T.B.escort being 955 K middle. From this point the route probably leads to Zeebrugge direct, but there is not enough positive evidence to state this definitely. 4' route has hardly been mentioned during the period dealt with." This gives some notion of the time lag.

166 Dorwart, op. cit., 126. For British reluctance to cooperate with American Military Intelligence see Yardley, *The American Black Chamber*, Chapter 10; Kahn, op. cit., 277; Beesly, op. cit., 179-81.

167 Marder, op. cit., 4.267.

168 Further problems with "*French indiscretions*," Andrew, *Her Majesty's Secret Service*, 124-25.

169 ADM 137/645.

170 Boucard, "Les secrets du chiffre," Gringoire 28 May 1937; Spindler, op. cit., 3.168, 342

171 T. Termote, *Verdwenen in de Noordzee*, 79-94.

172 Gayer, *Die Deutschen U-Boote*, 1.25; Thring in ADM 137/3912.

173 Bonatz, *Die Deutsche Marine-Funkaufklärung*, 30.

174 ADM 137/2274.

175 See McCartney, *Lost Patrols*, 148-49.

176 Spindler, op. cit., 2.44-45.

177 ADM 137/2096.

178 Termote, *Verdwenen in de Noordzee*, 95-96.

179 Spindler, op. cit., 2.222.

180 All details are found in ADM 137/1114: Lowestoft, Yarmouth and Harwich. Auxiliary Patrol Area X. Armed Smacks. Minesweeping. Various Subjects. 1915 July to December. Pp. 105-58. Sinking of Enemy s/m by S. S. *Cottingham* by collision in Stanford Channel 2/7/15 (with divers' report); others in ADM 137/3960: Messages Despatched from War Room, 3 Feb-5 Aug 1915.

181 Spindler, op. cit., 2.229.

182 Corbett, op. cit., 3.129; diver's sketch in *U-Boat Intelligence*, 14 (from ADM 137/1114).

183 These were E-24, E-34, E-41, E-45, E-46, and E-51.

184 ADM 137/3960; Spindler, op. cit., 2.226.

185 Gogg, *Österreichs Kriegsmarine*, 73 (no. 530). Several fragments from *UC10*, torpedoed by *E54* on the Steenbank in August 1916, bear the number "U22" (Termote, *Verdwenen in de Noordzee*, 103-6), and Gogg reports that *UC14* and *UC15* were numbered "18" and "19," while *UC13* was "25" (Gogg, 73). Evidently "U22" is a number intended for Austria. The German *UB1* became Austrian "U10" before being mined in shallow water near Caorlé on

July 9, 1918. Soon raised, the wreck was surrendered to Italy and broken up in 1920 (Gogg 72; http/uboat.net/wwi).

[186] Spindler, op. cit., 2.197; 3.46-47.

[187] Beesly, op. cit., 264; cf. "Masters," *When Ships Go Down*, 296.

[188] ADM 137/3876.

[189] ADM 137/3060.

[190] ADM 116/1504-5; cf. Robinson, op. cit., 136-37.

[191] ADM 137/451.

[192] ADM 137/3876.

[193] ADM 116/1424; a more dramatic account in "Masters," op. cit., 296-302.

[194] ADM 137/451.

[195] ADM 137/1408-10.

[196] Robinson, op. cit., 186.

[197] Letter of 14 January 1968, based on remarks by W. James. Did Peterson assume that flames destroyed codebooks?

[198] Beesly, op. cit., 27 and 145; Robinson, op. cit., 189.

[199] ADM 137/3964; copy of translation: 573; original: 362. The location must be Littlestone on Sea, about five miles north of Dungeness; evidently L-32 was looking for a landmark: Jones, War in the Air 3.227; 3 (Maps), map 39.

[200] ADM 116/1506.

[201] See Davis, *Deep Diving and Submarine Operations*, 242-57.

[202] ADM 137/2591.

[203] ADM 137/645.

[204] ADM 137/3869.

[205] Sinking and Ida, ADM 137/3897; paper, 3871.

[206] ADM 137/3875.

[207] ADM 137/4171.

[208] ADM 137/3898 (p.96).

[209] ADM 137/2096.

[210] ADM 137/645.

[211] ADM 137/2096, 3898.

[212] PG 62061.

[213] Hurd, *Merchant Navy*, 3.217; Gibson and Prendergast, op. cit., 196; James, op. cit.,116; Beesly, op. cit., 265.

[214] Churchill College Cambridge, Archives Centre HALL 2/1, "Rough Notes," p.4. Tebenjohanns himself related that he took a walk in South Kensington with Major Trench but answered no questions (Hashagen, U-Boats Westward, 127-28).

[215] ADM 137/3897.

[216] Spindler, op. cit., 4 Skizze 14B, Field 119a (wrongly marked on the chart).

[217] ADM 116/1632.

[218] ADM 137/645.

[219] ADM 137/645.

[220] AFB with "alterations": ADM 137/4248-49 (changes for May 31, June 20, August 20, September 20, October 23, November 25, 1917, and January 20, 1918); call signs: 137/4251-52.

[221] Orders: ADM 137/4261; neutrals: cf. Sims, *Victory at Sea*, 317.

[222] ADM 137/3886.

[223] Around 1960 part of it was in the Naval Historical Branch basement in the Old War Office, Whitehall.

[224] Hackmann, Seek and Strike, 63.

[225] ADM 137/645.

[226] ADM 116/1640.

[227] Newbolt, *Submarine and Anti-Submarine*, 226-30.

[228] Chatterton, *Valiant Sailormen*, 220.

[229] ADM 137/645.

[230] Spindler, op. cit., 4, Skizze 14A.

[231] Carney, "*Capture of U58*," 1401, 1403.

[232] Spindler, op. cit., 4.456.

[233] ADM 137/1379.

[234] ADM 116/2591.

[235] ADM 137/645; 116/1632.

[236] McCartney, *Lost Patrols*, 113.

[237] ADM 137/1382.

[238] Keyes, Naval Memoirs, 2.157.

[239] ADM 137/849; cf. Spindler, op. cit., 4.114.

[240] ADM 137/849, pp. 142-43: "Summarised Record of Passages by Hostile Submarines."

[241] Cf. Grant, *U-Boat Intelligence*, 81, 99.

[242] ADM 137/641.

[243] For locations see chart in Grant, op. cit., 96; but my locations for *UB103* and *UC50* are wrong, and *UC78* should be *UC79*. For a modern identification of *UB56*, McCartney, Lost Patrols, 152.

[244] Keyes, op. cit., 2.172-73.

[245] Spindler, op. cit., 5.48.

[246] Keyes, op. cit., 2.172.

[247] ADM 137/3900; documents in 4747.

[248] ADM 116/1643.

[249] *Mercantile Navy List and Maritime Directory*, 1925, p. 364; cf. J. J. Colledge, *Ships of the Royal Navy: An Historical Index* (Newton Abbot, 1970), 2.243.

[250] ADM 137/2100, pp. 530-53.

[251] ADM 116/1634, 1642.

[252] The story about Damant and Miller must be the one

erroneously told about *UB4* in Diver Magazine, September 1998. See J. D. Perkins, "The Gunner and the U-Boat" (1999) at http.//www.ukans.edu/..kansite/ww_one/naval/ub4.htm.

[253] McCartney, *Lost Patrols*, 150.

[254] PG 62061.

[255] McCartney, *Lost Patrols*, 153-54.

[256] ADM 137/506.

[257] ADM 116/1634.

[258] ADM 137/3899. This was Stephen King-Hall. While serving in Birmingham he had witnessed the destruction of *U15* (cf. My Naval Life, 98) and could doubtless exchange reminiscences. In 1920 he published a mildly lifelike romance entitled The Diary of a U-Boat Commander, using his French name "Étienne."

[259] ADM 137/3898.

[260] ADM 137/869.

[261] ADM 116/1634.

[262] Spindler, op. cit., 5.76.

[263] An imaginative description of supposed damage to *UC56* in Gibson and Prendergast, op. cit., 305.

[264] ADM 116/1634; gelignite: ADM 116/1643. Meanwhile the wreck of *UC49*, depth-charged off Dartmouth on August 8, may have been located in 29 fathoms by "observers from the Dartmouth Experimental Station" but was not further investigated (Daily Return, August 13).

[265] McCartney, *Lost Patrols*, 65-66.

[266] ADM 137/3900.

[267] ADM 116/1634.

[268] Ibid.

[269] Not Shipwash, against Spindler, op. cit., 5.101.

[270] ADM 116/1634.

[271] ADM 137/849.

[272] Halpern, Keyes Papers, 1.504,

[273] Navy Department, American Naval Planning Section, 293.

[274] ADM 116/1643; the two were the investigations of *UB33* and *UC11*.

[275] McCartney, *Lost Patrols*, 152-53.

[276] Ibid. 147-48.

[277] ADM 137/2100.

[278] McCartney, *Lost Patrols*, 156-57.

[279] ADM 116/1851.

[280] G. Lechner (in regard to another case), Marine-Rundschau 54 (1957), 33.

[281] ADM 137/3886.

282 McCartney, *Lost Patrols*, 146-47 and 154-55. Supposedly *UB78* attacked the transport, but that submarine's wreck, identified from propeller markings, lies in 5101/0117E (not W).

283 This buoy was in 510015/011928 (ADM 137/2101).

284 McCartney, *Lost Patrols*, 151-52.

285 Ibid. 154.

286 Letter from J. J. Schieffelin 9 January 1966.

287 Fürbringer, *Alarm! Tauchen!!*, 223.

288 ADM 137/4071.

289 Hall's gift: ADM 116/1851; documents: ADM 137/4225-38; AFB: ADM 137/4377.

290 Gibson and Prendergast, op. cit., 314.

291 Spindler, op. cit., 126-27.

292 See Spindler, *Handelskrieg* 5.122.

293 http/uboat.net/wwi

294 Robinson, op. cit., 332 n. 3.

295 ADM 116/1858.

296 ADM 137/3869.

297 Letter from Douglas Robinson, 5 June 1990.

298 ADM 137/964.

299 The last was *L56*, which "at the end of the raid...flew over Lowestoft and out to sea, her C. O. being quite disoriented" (letter from Douglas Robinson, 4 February 1990).

300 ADM 137/869.

301 Thanks to my daughter Susan Slattery for finding this.

302 Termote, *Verdwenen in de Noordzee*, 107-12.

303 Spindler, op. cit., 5.97.

304 PG 62062.

305 ADM 137/2100.

306 Leith, *British Minefields*, 168.

307 *UB103*: ADM 137/2097; Gris Nez: ADM 116/2012 (Item 14).

308 ADM 137/3900.

309 PG 61864.

310 ADM 137/869.

311 ADM 116/1851. The secret papers on *UB109* are listed in PG 69299.

312 ADM 137/3917.

313 The only document from *UB109's* last cruise now available seems to be ADM 137/4224: "Intercepted foreign messages" from July 27 to August 25.

314 ADM 116/1851.

315 On the sinking see Jones, *War in the Air*, 6.346-47.

316 ADM 116/1644.

317 PG 69299.

318 AFB and Tauschtafeln: ADM 137/4270; Funknamen, 4269.

[319] Radio signals: ADM 137/4267; notebook: 3898.

[320] Cf. Jones, op. cit., 6.347-48.

[321] No examination: ADM 116/1634; sweep: 1851; James: ADM 137/1469.

[322] http/uboat.net/wwi

[323] Spindler, "Scapa Flow," 31-32.

[324] Hackmann, op. cit., 67.

[325] ADM 137/964.

[326] ADM 116/1851.

[327] ADM 137/964.

[328] PG 61871.

[329] ADM 137/1851.

[330] For the same situation twenty-five years later, see J. H. Kemler, *The struggle for wolfram in the Iberian Peninsula June, 1942--June, 1944* (University of Chicago dissertation, 1949); D. L. Wheeler, "Portugal, the Wolfram Question, and World War II," Luso-Brazilian Review 23,1 (1986), 107-27; 23,2 (1986), 97-111.

[331] Givierge, *Au Service*, 762-63; Ostrovsky, *Eye of Dawn*, 247-49, cites French intercepts.

[332] All this is based on ADM 137/3863: "Wolfram Aug. 1917 to May 1918;" 812: "Capture of SS. *Erri Bero*;" and Beesly, op. cit., 191-200.

[333] Similarly S. Uchino tells of Japanese submarines that brought wolfram to Germany from Japan: "Die erfolgreiche Fahrt des japanesischen U-Bootes 'I-8,'" Marine-Rundschau 81 (1984), 224-27, especially 227.

[334] ADM 137/4155.

[335] The British government had vehemently protested in August 1915 when German destroyers shelled E-13, stranded in Danish waters, and killed fifteen of the crew.

[336] PG 61713.

[337] ADM 137/2097.

[338] Valentiner, *Terreur des mers*, 190.

[339] PG 61714, including explanatory letter of 15 May 1936; Valentiner, op. cit., 188.

[340] Ibid. 204.

[341] *Celandine*: ADM 53/37836; J-1: ADM 173/5844.

[342] ADM 137/1611. Graham Greene knew about it in 1935 (Journey Without Maps, 237-38); a photograph of the station in Maugham, Republic of Liberia, 3rd plate after p. 32. .

[343] PG 61708; cf. ADM 137/1611.

[344] Yancy, *Republic of Liberia*, 64-66; Welch, *Jet Lighthouse*, 54; even Wilson, *Liberia: Black Africa in Microcosm*. A more sober statement of facts was made by the Liberian author Nnamdi Azikiwe, Liberia in World Politics, 86-88.

345 PG 76468.

34 | 6 ADM 137/1608.

347 *Bombala*: ADM 137/4056; Gibraltar: 770; Dakar: 1608.

348 ADM 137/869.

349 ADM 173/5844.

350 PG 61708.

351 Spindler, op. cit., 5.237; Hashagen, *U-Boats Westward*, 174-75.

352 ADM 137/869.

353 PG 61626; cf. Walle, "Anwendung," 135 n. 90.

354 PG 61843.

355 ADM 137/1611.

356 Michelsen, *La guerre sous-marine*, 90-91.

357 Navy Department, *German Submarine Activities*, 9.

358 Ibid. 10.

359 American analysis, ibid. 119-21.

360 Goerlitz, *Kaiser and His Court*, 360.

361 Newbolt, *Naval Operations*, 5.340-41. Her position on July 7 was in 5053/2403, but by July 12 she had reached 5828/ 1029, moving on to 5943/0816 (southwest of the Faeroes) on the 13th, 6125/0348 (between the Faeroes and the Orkneys) on the 14th, 6133/0029 East (just northeast of the Orkneys) on the 15th, and Norwegian waters on the 16th.

362 Signals, ADM 137/3915; orders, ADM 137/1455.

363 ADM 137/1453.

364 PG 61705.

365 Thomas, *Raiders of the Deep*, 332.

366 Goerlitz, op. cit., 375.

367 ADM 137/4594.

368 Goerlitz, op. cit., 369.

369 James, *German Subs*, 82.

370 Darling, *French Cable Station*, 13, with suggestion of search for cable.

371 ADM 137/4594.

372 PG 61854.

373 Navy Department, *German Submarine Activities*, 63.

374 Birch, Contribution, 1.656.

375 PG 61854. This was from 5957N/0130E to 5921N/0242E.

376 ADM 173/7790; 137/1453.

377 C.-H. Ankarberg, "Search for a sunken U-boat," Shetland Fishing News No. 151 (May 1998), 15.

378 Canada, Department of National Defence Records RG 24/4021 -- Naval Service File 1062-13-2, vol. 5.

379 Goerlitz, op. cit., 404.

380 Bauer, *Unterseeboot*, 52.

381 Michelsen, *Guerre sous-marine*, 157.

382 The figure was reported by *U152*.

383 Clephane, *Naval Overseas Transportation Service*, 175-77.

384 Ibid. 173-75; Spindler, op. cit., 5.253-56.

385 Navy Department, *American Naval Planning Section*, 78-83.

386 National Archives (U. S.), RG 45, Box 185.

387 Editors of Navy Times, *They Fought Under the Sea*, 82.

388 Cf. H. C. Bywater in U. S. Naval Institute Proceedings 50 (1924), 460.

389 PG 61705.

390 Birch, op. cit., 1.660-61.

391 Navy Department, *German Submarine Activities*, 75.

392 His narrative appeared in the Standard Oil magazine The Lamp for April 1919.

393 ADM 137/1617.

394 Beckmann, *U-Boote vor New-York*, Plate IV; correct caption by von Langsdorff, U-Boote am Feind, opposite 208; he got the picture from Kurt Zachow, chief engineer of *U151*.

395 Niemoeller, *From U-Boat to Pulpit*, 81; a similar photo appears opposite p. 80.

396 Because *U117* finally ran out of oil and signalled for towing, it was wrongly supposed that she had assisted the leaking *U140* and later ran short of oil (Navy Department, *German Submarine Activities*, 82, 99-100; Clark, *When the U-Boats Came to America*, 249 ["forty-three gallons"!]; James, *German Subs*, 148).

397 Goerlitz, op. cit., 392.

398 Thomas, *Raiders of the Deep*, 335.

399 See Laurens, *Histoire de la guerre sous-marine*, 366-67, evidently based on the war diary of *U139*.

400 ADM 137/3915.

401 War Diary: ADM 53/55099.

402 K/K Pistor in Herzog, *60 Jahre*, 168 n. 4.

403 Thomas, op. cit., 340; cf. von Arnauld in Langsdorff, *U-Boote am Feind*, 76.

404 314 ADM 137/1453.

405 Laurens, op. cit., 367.

406 Beesly, op. cit., 255-56; ADM 137/645.

407 According to http//uboat.net/wwi/fates/losses.html she was mined on 21 April in 5520/0715E.

408 Ruge, *Im Küstenvorfeld*, 16; see the case of *U106*.

409 *UC32, UC33, UC41, UC42, UC44* (see Chapter 6).

410 There is a copy in Widener Library at Harvard.

411 Spindler, op. cit., 4.249.

412 National Archives RG 45, Box 186.

413 Newbolt, op. cit., 5.287.

[414] ADM 137/1583.

[415] Halpern, *Naval War in the Mediterranean*, 399.

[416] Goerlitz, *Kaiser and His Court*, 359.

[417] Grid-Tech-Diver at www.grid-tech-divers.com. My thanks to Wayne Messimer for this information.

[418] See E, K. Chatterton, *Beating the U-Boats* (London, 1943), 133, and Spindler, *Handelskrieg* 5.60, with list on p.404 including the names.

[419] Keyes, op. cit., 2.341.

[420] *U-Boats Destroyed*, 89; *U-Boat Intelligence*, 171.

[421] Spindler, op. cit., 5.38; but cf. 5.410 (O/L Eschweiler).

[422] PG 90891.

[423] Spindler, op. cit., 5.38.

[424] ADM 116/1632; cf. A.C. Dewar's note in C.B. 01292, OXO, Case 113 for 1918, and ADM 137/3917.

[425] As in http//uboat.net/wwi/fates//losses.html

[426] Navy Department, *The Northern Barrage*, 1.102-4.

[427] Cowie, *Mines*, 80.

[428] "Submarine Losses Return," C.B. 01292, OXO, 1918, #194.

[429] Letter of P.F. Foster to R.M. Grant, January 1939.

[430] RG 45, JU Box 218, *UB65* file.

[431] ADM 137/1453.

BIBLIOGRAPHY

I OFFICIAL MATERIALS

AMERICAN
DOCUMENTS
[Weekly, then] Daily reports from A C Naval Staff for Force Commander London (Vice Admiral Sims, U.S.N.) [In National Archives, Washington, Record Group 145, TG Box 557]

UNPUBLISHED OFFICIAL HISTORY
Cocke, H. C. *Brief History of the Office of Naval Intelligence.* Washington 1930 [In National Archives, Washington]

OFFICIAL PUBLICATIONS
Naval Investigation. *Hearings before the Subcommittee of the Committee on Naval Affairs, United States Senate. Sixty-sixth Congress,* Second Session, 2 vols. Washington 1921

Navy Department. The American Naval Planning Section in London. Washington 1923
---- *German Submarine Activities on the Atlantic Coast of the United States and Canada.* Washington 1920
---- *The Northern Barrage,* 2 vols. Washington 1920

BRITISH
DOCUMENTS
ADM 116 (salvage), 137 (operations and intelligence). Classifications of Admiralty documents in Public Record Office, London [see also PG (Abbreviations)]

Admiralty. *Diving Manual.* 1916 (Admiralty, G.24974/16)

----- *Submarine Losses Return.* C.B. 01292 A-G, O. X. O. January 1917-- November 1918 = Reported Destruction of Submarines. [In National Archives, Washington, and Naval Library, London.]

----- Dewar, A. C. *Notes on "Submarine Losses Return."* [In Naval Library, London]

----- Submarines' Tactical Formation August 4th 1914--April 30th 1917. ["This book was made primarily to enable Paymaster Commander Thring to work on Submarine W.T. Messages. The material for the early years was scant, and the book in consequence contains a great number of additions and corrections by Paymaster Commander Thring R. N."]

----- Trade Division, Naval Staff. *War Instructions for British Merchant Ships* (C.B. No. 415). August 1917. ["This book is weighted with lead, and if thrown overboard will sink."]

UNPUBLISHED OFFICIAL HISTORIES
Birch, F., and Clarke, W. F. *Contribution to the History of German Naval Warfare 1914-1918*. London 1919-1922 [In Naval Library, London]
Leith, L. *The History of British Minefields 1914-1918*. London 1920 [In Naval Library, London]

OFFICIAL HISTORIES
Corbett, J. S. *Naval Operations I-III*. London 1920-1923.
Newbolt, H. *Naval Operations* IV-V. London 1928, 1931
Fayle, C.E., *Seaborne Trade I-III*. London 1920-1924
Hurd, A. *The Merchant Navy I-III*. London 1921-1929
Jones, H. A. *The War in the Air II-VI*. Oxford 1928-1937

FRENCH
UNPUBLISHED DOCUMENTS
Ministère de la Marine. *Direction Générale de la guerre sous-marine. Section des renseignements-Etat-Major Général. 1re section. Étude des Mouvements et Actes des sous-marins ennemis.* Paris 1916-1918. (In Sterling Library, Yale University)

UNPUBLISHED OFFICIAL HISTORIES

. Givierge, P. *Au service du chiffre*. (In Bibliothèque Nationale, Paris, Département des Mss., Don 18899)
---- *Étude historique sur le section du Chiffre (1889-1921) I-III*. (In Bibliothèque Nationale, Paris, Département des Mss., N. A. F. 24.353-24.355)

GERMAN
DOCUMENTS
National Archives Microfilm Publications: Microcopy No. T-1022
Guides to the Microfilmed Records of the German Navy, 1850-1945: No. 1. U-Boats and T-Boats 1914-1918. Washington 1984

PUBLISHED OFFICIAL HISTORIES

Groos, O. *Der Krieg in der Nordsee, I-V.* Berlin 1922-1925; Vol. VI by Gladisch, W. Berlin 1937. VII. Frankfurt/Main 1965
Lorey, H. *Der Krieg in den türkischern Gewässern, I-. II.* Berlin 1928, 1938

Spindler, A. *Der Handelskrieg mit U-Booten I-IV.* Berlin 1932-1941 (vol. IV, repr. Hamburg 1965); Vol. V. Frankfurt/Main 1966

II INDIVIDUAL WORKS

Andrew, C. *Her Majesty's Secret Service: The Making of the British Intelligence Community.* New York 1986
Ankarberg, C.-H. "Search for a sunken U-boat," Shetland Fishing News No. 151 (May 1998), 15 [U156]
Anonymous. "A War Secret," Saturday Evening Post, October 23, 1926
Anonymous. "Submarine Episodes," The Seagoer 1937, 87-97
Azikiwe, N., Liberia in World Politics. London 1934
Babbs, E. "The Sinking of U. B. 109," Journal of the Royal United Service Institution 81 (1936), 185
Bacon, R. H. The Dover Patrol. 2 vols., New York, 1919
Bacon The Concise Story of the Dover Patrol. London
    1932
Bastin, R. H. "Dodging the Ashcans in a Pirate Submersible: Standard Oil Sailor's Adventures Outrival Verne," The Lamp, April 1919, 5-9
Bauer, H. *Das Unterseeboot: Seine Bedeutung als Teil einer Flotte Seine Stellung im Völkerrecht Seine Kriegsverwendung Seine Zukunft.* Berlin 1931
Bauermeister, H. "Die Entwicklung der Magnetminen bis zum Beginn des Zweiten Weltkrieges," Marine-Rundschau 55 (1958), 25-31
Beesly, P. *Room 40: British Naval Intelligence 1914-1918.* London 1982
---- "Das Signalbuch der 'Magdeburg' half den Ersten Weltkrieg zu gewinnen," Marine-Rundschau 78
    (1981), 273-76
Belknap. R. R. *The Yankee Mining Squadron.* Annapolis: 1920
Bird, K. *German Naval History: a guide to the literature.* New York 1985
Bonatz, H. Die deutsche Marine-Funkaufklärung 1914-1945. Darmstadt 1970
Boucard, R. "Les secrets du chiffre," Gringoire 28 May 1937
Bright, C. "Telegraphs in War Time," The Nineteenth Century and After 77 (1915), 861-78
Brown, F. J., *The Cable and Wireless Communications of the World. London* 1927
Bywater, H. C. *Their Secret Purposes.* London 1932

Bywater, H. C. and H. C. Ferraby. *Strange Intelligence: Memoirs of Naval Secret Service*. London 1931, 1934

Carney, R. B. "The Capture of the *U58*," United States Naval Institute Proceedings 60 (1934), 1401-4

Chatterton, E. K. Beating the U-Boats. London 1943 [1917-1918]

Chatterton E. K. *Fighting the U-Boats*. London 1942 [1914-1916]

Chatterton E. K. *Q-Ships and their Story*. London 1922

Chatterton E. K. *Valiant Sailormen*. London 1936

Clark, W. B. *When the U-Boats Came to America*. Boston 1929

Clarke, W. F. "Government Code and Cypher School: Its Foundation and Development with Special Reference to its Naval Side," Cryptologia 11 (1987), 218-26

Clarke, W. F. "The Years Between," ibid. 12 (1988), 52-58

Clarke, W. F. "Bletchley Park 1941-1945," ibid. 90-97

Clarke, W. F. "Post War Organization," ibid. 174-77

Cowie, J. S. *Mines, Minelayers and Minelaying, 2nd ed.* London 1949

Darling, W. S. *The French Cable Station Museum*.Orleans MA 1988

Davis, Robert Henry. *Deep Diving and Submarine Operations.* 6th ed., London c. 1955

Dorwart, J. M. *The Office of Naval Intelligence*. Annapolis 1979

Erskine, R. "The German Naval Grid in World War II," Cryptologia 16 (1992), 39-51

Ewing, A. W. *The Man of Room 40: The Life of Sir Alfred Ewing.* London c. 1939

Fitzgerald, P. *The Knox Brothers*. London 1977

Fürbringer, W. *Alarm! Tauchen!! U-Boot in Kampf und Sturm.* Berlin 1933 [*UB110*]

Gayer, A. *Die deutschen U-Boote in ihrer Kriegsfuehrung, 1914-1918.* 4 vols., Berlin 1920-1930 [only to February 1917]

Gibson, R. H., and Prendergast, M. *The German Submarine War*, 2nd ed. London 1931; repr. Penzance: Periscope Publishing 2002

Gilbert, M. (continuator of Churchill, R. S.), *Winston S. Churchill, III* (1914-1916). London 1971

Gogg, K. *Österreichs Kriegsmarine 1848-1918.* Salzburg, 1967

Grant, R. M. *U-Boat Intelligence.* London 1969; repr. Penzance: Periscope Publishing 2002

Grant, R. M *U-Boats Destroyed.* London 1964; repr. Penzance: Periscope Publishing 2002

Graves, C. *The Thin Red Lines*. London [1946]

Greene, G. *Journey Without Maps*. London 1936 (Penguin reprint, 1971)

Hackmann, W. *Seek and Strike. Sonar, anti-submarine warfare and the Royal Navy 1914-54.* London 1984

Halpern, P. G. *The Naval War in the Mediterranean, 1914-1918.* Annapolis 1987

Halpern, P. G ed. *The Keyes Papers I-III.* London 1972-1981

Harbord, J. G. *The American Army in France 1917-1919.* Boston 1936

Hartmann, G. K. *Weapons that Wait: Mine Warfare in the U.S. Navy.* Annapolis 1979

Hashagen, E. *U-Boats Westward.* New York 1931

James, H. J. *German Subs in Yankee Waters: First World War.* New York 1940

James, W. *The Code Breakers of Room 40.* New York 1956

Jeschke, H. *U-Boottaktik: Zur deutschen U-Boottaktik 1900-1945.* Freiburg 1972

Jones, R. V. *The Wizard War: British Scientific Intelligence 1939-1945.* New York 1978

Jordan, G. (ed.). *Naval Warfare in the Twentieth Century 1900-1945. Essays in honour of Arthur Marder.* London--New York 1977

Kahn, D. *The Codebreakers: The Story of Secret Writing.* New York 1967

Kahn, D. *Kahn on Codes.* New York c. 1983 [pp. 286-87]

Kahn, D. *Seizing the Enigma. The Race to Break the German U-Boat Codes.* Boston 1991

Kemp, P. K. *H. M. Submarine.* London 1952

Keyes, R. *The Naval Memoirs II: Scapa Flow to the Dover Straits 1916-1918.* New York 1935 (See Halpern, P. G.)

King-Hall, S. *My Naval Life 1906-1929.* London 1952

Larn, R. *Goodwin Sands Shipwrecks.* London 1977

Leighton, J. L. *Simsadus:* London. New York 1920

Lundeberg, P. K. "The German Naval Critique of the U-Boat Campaign, 1915-1918," Military Affairs 27 (1963), 105-16

Lundeberg, P. K. "Undersea Warfare and Allied Strategy in World War I," Smithsonian Journal of History 1.3 (1966), 1-30; 1.4 (1967), 49-72

Mäkelä, M. *Das Geheimnis der "Magdeburg".* Coblenz 1984

Marder, A. J. *From the Dreadnought to Scapa Flow III-V.* London 1966-1970

Masters, D. (C. E. Brand). *The Wonders of Salvage* London 1924

Masters, D. *When Ships Go Down.* London, 1932

Maugham, R. C. F. *The Republic of Liberia.* London-New York 1920

McCartney, Innes. *Lost Patrols: Submarine Wrecks of the English Channel.* Penzance: Periscope Publishing 2003

Messimer, D. R. *Verschollen: World War I U-Boat Losses.* Annapolis 2002

Michelsen, A. *La guerre sous-marine.* Paris 1928

Millais, G. *Sir John Everett Millais.* London 1979

Moraht, R. *Werwolf der Meere: "U64" jagt den Feind.* Berlin 1933

Newbolt, H. *Submarine and Anti-Submarine.* London 1918

Ostrovsky, E. *Eye of Dawn: The Rise and Fall of Mata Hari.* New York 1978

Pearson, J. *The Life of Ian Fleming.* New York 1966

Robinson, D. H. *The Zeppelin in Combat 1912-1918* London 1962

Rosenberg, B. A., and A. H. Stewart. *Ian Fleming.* Boston 1989

Roskill, S. *Hankey: Man of Secrets, 1.* London 1970

Rössler, E. *Geschichte des deutschen Ubootbaus.* Munich 1975

Rowan, R. W. *The Story of Secret Service.* New York 1939

Ruge, F. *Im Küstenvorfeld.* 2nd ed., Munich 1977

Sansoni, A. "The First Ultra Secret: the British Cryptanalysis in the Naval Operations of the First World War," Revue Internationale d'histoire militaire 63 (1985), 99-110

Sims, W. S. *The Victory at Sea.* New York 1920

Spindler, A. "Herr Hector Bywater bringt Dramatisches von deutschen U-Booten," Marine-Rundschau 38 (1933), 412-13

Spindler, A "Scapa Flow -- Ziel deutscher U-Bootsangriffe," Marine-Rundschau 36 (1931), 27-34

Tarrant, V. E. *The U-Boat Offensive 1914-1945.* Annapolis c. 1989

Termote, T. *Verdwenen in de Noordzee.* Belgium: De Krijer 1999

Terraine, J. Business in Great Waters. *The U-Boat Wars 1916-1945.* London 1989

Tuchman, B. *The Zimmermann Telegram.* New York 1958

Valentiner, M., *La terreur des mers: Mes aventures en sous-marin 1914-1918.* Paris 1931

Waldeyer-Hartz, H. von. *Admiral von Hipper.* London 1933

Walle, H. "Die Anwendung der Funktelegraphie beim Einsatz deutschen U-Boote im Ersten Weltkrieg," Revue Internationale d'histoire militaire 63 (1985), 111-38

Welch, G. *The Jet Lighthouse.* London 1960

Wilson, C. M. *Liberia: Black Africa in Microcosm.* New York 1971

Wright, P. *The Republic of Liberia.* London 1959

Yardley, H. O. *The American Black Chamber.* London 1931

INDEX

U18, 136
U20, 138
U23, 137
U26, 137
U27, 32, 137
U28, 140
U29, 137
U31, 42, 43, 136
U32, 143
U34, 145
U35, 42, 124
U36, 137
U37, 43, 137
U38, 16, 132
U39, 144
U41, 137
U44, 129, 130, 140
U45, 19, 140
U48, 130, 141
U49, 17, 140
U50, 18, 21, 36, 128, 140
U51, 138
U53, 16, 60
U54, 19
U56, 138
U58, 62, 141, 155, 165
U59, 139
U61, 143
U64, 27, 144, 166
U66, 19, 140
U68, 137
U69, 140
U74, 138
U75, 21, 141
U76, 138
U77, 138
U78, 145
U81, 139
U83, 139
U84, 129, 142
U85, 139
U87, 142
U88, 19, 21, 140
U89, 142

U92, 145
U93, 142
U94, 36, 129
U95, 142
U99, 140
U101, 69
U102, 145
U103, 143, 148, 149
U104, 143
U105, 130
U106, 20, 21, 141, 160
U109, 65, 66, 142
U110, 142
U117, 115, 120, 121, 123, 124, 160
U139, 114, 115, 116, 120, 121, 124,
    125, 126, 127, 160
U140, 114, 115, 120, 121, 122, 123,
    124, 125, 127, 160
U151, 110, 111, 112, 115, 119, 121,
    123, 160
U152, 103, 114, 116, 117, 118, 119,
    126, 160
U153, 37, 103, 105, 106, 107, 109
U154, 13, 103, 104, 105, 106, 107,
    108, 109, 143
U155, 16, 99, 110, 117, 118, 126
U156, 16, 37, 99, 100, 101, 103, 109,
    112, 113, 114, 115, 116, 117, 118,
    122, 124, 125, 145, 164
U157, 16, 37, 99, 100, 102, 103, 126
U161, 115
UB1, 144
UB3, 137
UB4, 137
UB6, 139
UB7, 138
UB12, 144
UB13, 137
UB14, 33
UB16, 68, 143
UB17, 142
UB18, 49, 141
UB19, 138
UB20, 79, 140

OTHER BOOKS BY PERISCOPE PUBLISHING

Available from www.periscopepublishing.com

U-BOATS DESTROYED - by Robert M. Grant

U-BOAT INTELLIGENCE – by Robert M. Grant

LOST PATROLS – Submarine Wrecks of the English Channel – by Innes McCartney

THE GERMAN SUBMARINE WAR 1914-18 – by R. H. Gibson & Maurice Prendergast

RAIDERS OF THE DEEP – by Lowell Thomas

MY MYSTERY SHIPS – by Gordon Campbell VC

THE LIFE OF A Q-SHIP CAPTAIN – by Gordon Campbell VC

Q-BOAT ADVENTURES – by Harold Auten VC

ENCYCLOPAEDIA OF BRITISH SUBMARINES – by Paul Akermann

A SUBMARINER'S STORY – by Joel Blamey DSC DSM

DREADNOUGHT – Britain's First Nuclear Powered Submarine – by Patrick Boniface

THE BIG BATTLESHIP – The Story of HMS *Agincourt* – by Richard Hough

FALKLANDS 1914 – The Pursuit of von Spee – by Richard Hough

ADMIRALS IN COLLISION – by Richard Hough

DREADNOUGHT – A History of the Modern Battleship – by Richard Hough

THE FIGHTING TENTH – by John Wingate

BRITISH SUBMARINERS IN WW1 – by Richard MacKay